T0146938

My Italian Angel

Lotte Søs Farran-Lee

BALBOA.
PRESS

A DIVISION OF HAY HOUSE

Balboa Press books may be ordered through booksellers or by contacting:

Balboa Press
A Division of Hay House
1663 Liberty Drive
Bloomington, IN 47403
www.balboapress.com
1 (877) 407-4847

Print information available on the last page.

ISBN:978-1-5043-8696-8 (sc)
ISBN: 978-1-5043-8725-5 (e)

Balboa Press rev. date: 08/23/2017

Contents

ONE

The Fucked Up Soul

She had fucked-up! That was for sure…Her actions had riddled her soul with pain, but she felt that there was simply no choice: she had to do it.

…She had purposely fallen in love with a man but not just any man: her therapist! It had been a conscious decision and it wasn't about becoming his lover, but to get closer to the pain she felt so deeply within her soul.

That pain… she couldn't recall a day in her life where it hadn't felt like a shadow hanging over her constantly reminding her in every situation of life how different she was from every one else. At times, it felt like she had jumped into the wrong theater play, like she was supposed to be in an entirely different one, a play where she didn't constantly feel like she was from another planet.

She was married, married to Mads and he was fantastic, so why on earth had she put herself in this situation? She felt like an idiot and a fraud, but the only thing she really wanted was to get rid of that pain, so she could get closer to her husband, so she could learn how to love and be loved more deeply.

She felt that deep within she did know how to love with passion and depth, but that it needed to surface somehow and her mission was finding the key to unlock it.

In order to heal she had desperately gone to many different kinds of healing and therapist processes over the years and every time challenging herself more and more. The therapists had talked a lot about love, the unconditional love, but when she had expressed her feelings and the longing in herself to meet that part, they had all failed to guide her to that encounter.

They had just spoken the beautiful words devoid of any direction as to how to bring that into a reality. They were all afraid of actively showing that love in action. The big love… the love that connects us all.

She felt they were all frauds.

Only owning words without substance.

But no courage to live it.

She thought she had control when planning the falling in love thing.

Was she wrong?

Oh YES!

Very wrong.

And boy had she fucked up… Her soul, her biggest pain in life had just become even greater and now she had to face the fact that she had put herself in a situation where she was again so different to all others and not just a little different but majorly.

She felt something had changed within her system. It was the flood of feelings within her that had truly become uncontrollable, so much so that a therapist just wouldn't be enough any longer, she needed a teacher, a wise teacher.

The worst part was that she didn't know where to go and she was too scared to talk to anyone about it. She wanted to call someone and say: "I fucked up my soul". But who to call? The phonebook didn't respond to fucked up soul's or at least the phonebook she had.

She knew what had happened to her in that the falling in love part with her therapist. She had woken up her soul, her full potential; the problem was that only her mind was accepting it and not her body.

It felt like she had built a rocket that could be taken into space to discover the truth.

Her innermost truth of how she fitted into the grand plan of life and all she had to do was to learn how to love unconditionally. That was her lesson.

But how on earth do you learn that?

Therapy felt to narrow to even bringing small parts of that learning process in the light to be learned.

But she was in the shit, she knew. The feeling of her mind being so open, so open that she felt that she was loosing it. Loosing her mind. That part had not been a part of her plan.

She could hear herself when taking to her friends that she was not in a good place, she spoke about love, she spoke about that energy…the energy that she felt in herself that had gone so terribly wrong. The energy of the rocket that was out of control… none of it made sense to anyone she knew.

Katrin was terrified; terrified that she had fucked up her soul so badly that she would never be able to return to something that she could call even the slightest bit normal. Not that she had ever felt normal in her life, but now… it was so out of hand, so non-reachable that she doubted that she could ever be… or feel… just a little bit… like she belonged here too… here on earth.

What was the way back?
Or was there a way back?
Back to her.
But she didn't even like going back.
She wanted to be her.
Now everything was fucked.
So fucked up.
She hung onto something.
Hung to the little…
That little crack of light.
That little crack of hope.
Were the equation was.
Learning how to love.
Then she would be home with herself.

She knew it sounded like an impossible task to solve, but the thought of loosing her mind was not an option. She was not destined to be locked up with others that had lost their mind. She wanted to be whole, she wanted to be her.

Katrin went to see a healer one day… She had said to him that she had fucked up her soul, that something had happened to her. She felt like it was an awaking to her soul. An awakening that the Indian's would call Kundalini. She didn't much care about the name given to the experience.

He had said, "I can heal you".

She had told him to get his hands off.

She had just wanted confirmation that she was right.

That it was a spiritual awakening.

That she had fucked up her soul.

He didn't agree that she had fucked up.

He said it was beautiful.

She felt it was hell.

A common mistake of healers.

Or that was her opinion.

That hell was seen to be beautiful when covered in some spiritual name.

She felt that was a lie.

She had gone to the woods, felt Mother nature in her system when hugging the trees, smelling the earth. She wanted to disappear, disappear in the woods, letting Mother nature absorb her and not let her back into reality.

It was as if God had heard her prayers or at least someone with her email address, because out of the blue a body therapy seminar was due to be held in Northern Ireland. She knew… she had to go. Every time a little light felt brighter at a place she had to go. She had to follow the small trails being put out in front of her.

She was of course always arguing with herself about the logical side of it every time those hunches and nudges to attend came about… but in the end she always did it.

It was about control.

She wanted to go one way, get the damage she had done undone. Fix it and then return to the life she had created so far.

Was that possible?
No.

Was she about to get surprised?
And out of control?
Yes, indeed!

She was on the train, heading towards a small town in Northern Ireland. Katrin had been attending seminars for quite some time now. She had found some that really made a difference.

She was travelling a lot.

Taking classes in Europe, north, south, east, west… wherever. As long as the pain became a little bit milder every time, she was happy.

It felt, that it was not just about learning new information, but also that the travel itself offered valuable knowledge or valuable friendships for her.

There was an Italian woman onboard the train, she glanced at her, and could see that she was checking her out; she felt that this woman would also be on the seminar she was heading to.

"Where are you going?" The Italian lady asked.
"I'm going to a bed and breakfast".
"I knew it was you when I saw you".
"What do you mean?"
"I knew a Dane was coming, and I could just sense it was you".
"Are we going the same place?"

"Yes, we are".

"That is so great. I know the guy from the bed and breakfast is coming to get us".

"Yes, he is here with his car".

They started talking about where they came from, family etc. Once people started talking, she had the ability to sense their whole life, their energy and their pain. The Italian woman, Rosa, began to talk about her whole family and her mother who she was living with momentarily. How intense she found her and the arguments they were having.

She felt a touch of craziness from Rosa. It scared her a bit; she didn't want to get that involved with her, or be part of too much drama. She could instantly see the woman's life. She was doing a lot of meditation she said. She would go to retreats and meditate for days.

Katrin herself, did a little morning meditation, but doing it for days!! - too intense for her, and also too boring. She liked to move, do stuff, get somewhere, create...

They helped each other out of the train. It was dark when they arrived at a station called Cullybackey, he was here, their B&B guy. It was easy to see him.

He was a bit agitated, seemed nervous but wanted to be very gentle and took their bags, making sure everything was okay. He asked them questions all the time while driving back and explaining every detail. At the same time he was telling them the story of the small city they were in. He wanted to talk, and his need for company was huge.

He was lonely, it was easy to tell.

They were coming closer to the B&B, and they were now able to see the enormous old villa. Beautiful.

"Here we are" he said, watching them to see their reaction.
"Beautiful".
"Bellissimo".
They had the view of the field as it was built high on a hill.

"Come".

He opened the car door and stepped out, he was eager and proud. This was his home.

They all went straight up the stairs to the first floor. Rosa got the room on the left. Katrin got the big one on the right. It had a huge bed in the middle and a window in front of it. It was overlooking the fields and the valley with all the trees that they had just driven through. It wasn't just beautiful, it was full of character. She could hear Rosa and the B&B guy talking, they were bonding, and she didn't really feel the need. She could hear Rosa asking for a Body therapy session from him and as they were talking and talking their voices faded into the distance as her mind went off.

"So now I'm here…. It feels anxious. I feel anxious, and I think they are very intense. There is something quite beautiful here, and yet so unsolved, like people want to escape from here. But he loves it here, and he wants everyone else to love it as much as he does. It feels overwhelming here. I wonder what it is that I have to bring home with me this time? It's a bit creepy here, and so beautiful, but at the core of it, something is very wrong. I want to run away, but I also know I have to stay… I just want to be alone".

But it was not easy to be left alone in this place.

Soon there was knocking on the door.

"Do you want a cup of tea?"

In fact she did.

They went downstairs into the kitchen. Rosa came too.
There was stuff and pictures everywhere.
Katrin was glancing and sensing the place, always amazed when people could live with so much stuff. She noticed all the pictures around. It was clear that other women had lived there before.

There were pictures of different women all around, but of one woman in particular – she had red curly hair. She could feel that this woman had been a great love.

Later on he told them, that he had had three wives – all had left him.

She could sense that he was just looking for the next one to come, to fill in the gap, so he would not have to feel the loneliness inside him.

In a split second she felt a bit sorry for him, but as soon as he sensed that, he began talking and talking, and she quickly shut him out again.

He called for them, dinner was ready.
It was pitch dark outside.
Katrin and Rosa came downstairs.
There was a round table.
She was still amazed at all the stuff that was everywhere.

They talked and talked and right now he was kind, they all had a good time.

He spoke about a trip – he was going long distance.

To visit his son who was living on the other side of this big round ball, we call the earth.

She liked him, when he didn't try to please her and Rosa all the time.

When he just talked about what he liked.

He was so passionate about the Zero Point field - quantum science.

When he started to talk she felt his passion for this field, the field that connects us all. The physics of the; we're one. She was studying him while he was talking and she felt his passion really deep within her, and in that reflection, she felt her own passion for it, even though she didn't understand it. She knew that knowledge was important for her pain.

She went back upstairs, what a strange evening it had been and not just the evening really. It was a very intense journey this one. She felt scared, scared of not being with anyone she felt comfortable with, in a house that felt so painful and full of dead souls.

The feeling of being in a ghost house, was absolute. Katrin "shut down" her senses, didn't want to feel them. Other people loved to talk to dead ones. She didn't. What's the point really? They are dead and there is enough to deal with here on earth. She often felt and saw shadows, but she didn't want have anything to do with them.

Someone had once told her, that she could choose for herself if she wanted it or not.

She didn't need it her life.

But still, "they" were there.

Like someone who was attending a party they had not been asked to join.

"I really don't like it here, but I have to be here, I can't leave. And the feeling scares me. Someone is in the room. I will hide under the duvet, then at least I can't see them".

But she could feel them. They were strong, not evil, but many. They were pacing the room from left to the right. She was counting down – only three nights.

Her alarm went off, sun had arisen, morning had arrived.

"Thank God, it's morning".

Katrin felt anxious and excited too. She wanted her inner pain to shift, to leave her, and hoped that this time she could release more of it, but she was nervous too.

She remembered a song somebody once mentioned "they never promised you a rose garden". That was exactly how she felt. She wanted the rose garden, but whom did she really think had made her that promise? Just because she was born… But they were so many in the same shoes… 7 billion people?

She left her room and first thing the Italian woman commented on was her wet hair, like it was a catastrophe to have wet hair, inside a house.

She came down and saw the large breakfast feast. He had bought the whole supermarket for them, five different jams, yoghurt, different kind of breads, eggs, bacon… it went on and on.

"Do you want coffee?"

"Or do you want tea?"

"You could also get juice?"

"Or water?"

"Or, or, or…"

His questions went on and on. Rosa didn't want any breakfast, he was disappointed you could tell, he just wanted to do his best, and get positive feedback.

He got none.

Instead they got annoyed with him – both women.

Tried both to be polite.

He just wanted to be sweet, but it was all too much.

Katrin shut off again, could hear Rosa and him in the background, while she was staring out on the field. They started talking about the session he had given her yesterday.

She was glad she had stayed out.

The seminar started and she was excited, it was a nice group.

The two days were intense, not only because she was in this strange bed and breakfast, but the seminar too. One exercise in particular really captured her.

They had been asked to feel the inside of their body, their heart, lungs, stomach, hands, arm, legs, blood vessels, where they were tense, or relaxed; just observing and feeling. Then they had to feel the outside of their body, the skin surrounding them, lips, hair …. Then they were asked to expand outside the body and feel all the space. Finally they were asked to feel where their bodies began and where they ended. Does your body have a beginning? Does your body have an ending? Do you have a beginning or an ending?

"*I feel my body, I feel I'm tense in my shoulders, my heart is beating, I'm feeling my stomach, my breasts, my arms, I can feel all the blood running around in the arteries. I feel, my body, and I feel all the space that I am, the endless space that is here, where do I begin, where do I end. It feels like everything is just space, and now I'm just sitting here with my pumping heart and I feel that this is it, this is the most important part of the whole. My heart, no thoughts, just the awareness of my pumping heart. Like my body has vanished, everything. I feel that I found my gift here, my heart, that this is the center of my being, the rest of it, all this outside is not important. I have found the seat of my soul*".

She felt like she was born again. Felt proud of herself. She now knew why she absolutely had to go to this seminar, she had found her gift. Her heart.

Katrin was relieved when she parted from the Italian woman in the airport. The weekend had been intense, Rosa even more so, not to mention the B&B man. Boy had that been exhausting. But she was going home with a huge gift, her heart. In the end she had always done what she needed to do, but never felt a clear sense of what her heart wanted.

She felt a bit new, like she had been given a new chapter of her life. Of course it didn't happen as fast as she wanted it to, but every new wisdom, felt good. It felt like she was on the right track. The track of getting rid of this pain that she had. Because… damn that one that had hurt her, more than anything in the world.

She had often thought of it. Life was unfolding in a mysterious way. One event was leading to another, a mix of links that included people, events and experiences. It was a journey, like in a play, where she was playing her part. It was as if she had been in many plays, and right now this was an extremely important play in her life. The preparation part, the learning part of her life. She felt it had taken too long.

And she knew it was not over yet. This time felt crucial. She was learning and preparing herself for a very important part in her life. She was a fighter and she didn't give up, even though sometimes she wanted to but she just couldn't. She loved life too much. Wanted to live it to the fullest and her grandest potential. Even in this play of life that she was living right now. She knew she could do it; she just had to trust her own voice, now more than ever. She could not let that voice down. If she did that, she could no longer feel the purpose of her life.

TWO

Interrail

"Stop!"

"Stop!"

"Wait for me…"

"I'm here".

Her friend could hardly breathe but was laughing at the same time as she was stumbling forward. She had run all the way with her big bag pack. They were about to take the train… The second time she was going on her own out into the world. Maybe it was the same situation for her friend.

They were eighteen.

The ticket said Interrail.

They were loud and boisterous.

They found their seats and sat down on the train… checking out the carriage. They were going to be here for a long time.

The travel plan was a non-existent part of their travel kit.

They were sweating and laughing. So excited to go. Three men around their own age sat a bit further down in the carriage.

The whistles blew, the noise of the slamming doors, they pulled backed in their seats. Smiled.

Katrin closed her eyes and took a deep breath. Listened to the other people on the train chatting vaguely in the background then sank into her own world.

"How did I end up here? And with this friend? I don't know her that well, but she is really fun to be with. It's nice to get away and leave my broken heart behind. This trip will help me to get over it. I'm so tired of this place. Why am I born here in Denmark? I feel like a stranger. It's nice to leave it behind me, leave the country. It has been a really good year at school, but still, I'm so looking forward to leaving."

She opened her eyes and looked at her friend, quietly they looked out the window as the train was slowly pulling out of the train station. The train moved slowly out of the city and she was watching the houses and the people in the streets pass by the window, as the train slowly speeded up... Off to Europe.

Destination south.
They came from the north – Denmark.
They wanted the sun and the bikinis were packed.
Ready to party!

They started to look at the map, where should they go? They hadn't packed a tent, just a sleeping bag. Her friend had said that they could just sleep under the trees in their sleeping bag.

At this point in her life, she was not very skilled at judging what was practical and what was not, it was simply non-existent; she always followed the flow of life.

"Where do you think we should go?"

"Oh, let me see the map".

"Let's go somewhere warm".

"Yeah".

"Do you like France?"

"Yes, but I have been going there a lot my whole childhood, so I want something new".

"I understand… I don't like Spain".

"Yeahhhh, I don't quite feel for that either".

"Hmm… What about Italy?"

"Yes, that should be a really amazing place".

"What do you think? Milano? Venice?... Rome?... Ahhhh no, what about Florence, it should be marvelous?"

"Yes that sounds perfect, we just need to figure out, how to get there".

They had a big timetable of all the Interrail trains in Europe.

Katrin was really fascinated by this book. Instead of the familiar train stations, like Østerbro, Hellerup, Holte, this one listed stations in Berlin, Paris, Hamburg, Munchen, Milan, Rome, you could go on and on. It was so exciting and she felt like she had the whole world in front of her, just waiting to be explored.

They started to relax, knowing that they had to be here for quite a long time. Took out some snacks and started small talking. Her friend had just met a guy and there was so much to talk about.

They were heading for Hamburg.

The three guys came over, they were going to Corfu in Greece – they were Interrailers as well.

They all started talking and drinking. They got drunk and as the evening wore on she and one of the guys starting kissing.

She was tired and happy when they arrived in Florence the next morning. But glad to get away from those guys and happy to greet the morning sun of Italy.

They didn't say goodbye.

The smell and the warmth of Italy hit their bodies. It was so good to get out of the train. They sat down at a café. Got a coffee and a croissant.

"Mmmmmm, yes I like it here".

"We should have a walk around, and then go to the camping".

"Yes I would like to stay here in Florence".

"What a night! I'm glad we got away from those guys, why did I kiss that guy?"

They laughed.

They were walking around in Florence. It was a fantastic city, but they started to get really annoyed with the Italian men. They were so pushy. Every time they passed someone, they were hit on.

"It's overwhelming, they are really, really annoying, I don't like it. It scares me, they are really aggressive".

The two young women arrived at the camp grounds. They wanted a spot where they could sleep in their sleeping bags.

"You can't stay here without a tent".
"What?"

They looked at each other.

"I had the feeling, that we should have brought it with us. Why didn't I listen to my self? Shit, what to do now?"

"What should we do? Where should we go?"
"Maybe we should go to Rome, let's take it from there. There must be another town, where we can sleep without a tent. You said that right? That we could stay here without a tent?"
"Yes there must be a place, one of my friends told me that".

Anxiety was not really an issue, but they got angry instead and took it out on Italy. Like it was a stupid place, the Italian's were stupid, everything was stupid. All because of a damn tent.

Maybe it's needless to say, but they were young. Taking responsibility for their own actions was not the first choice.

So, they headed towards Rome. The wheels were whining when the breaks from the train forced the train to stop.

They got off the train, it felt like chaos. "Roma Termini" it said.

Katrin stood there for a while with all the bags, tired, exhausted, sweating and dirty. She wanted a bed, a real bed. Her friend had gone to the toilet. She observed the madness at the station, the noise, and all the people running around in the mess.

She glanced around. Her eyes stopped at another couple of eyes in the madness. He was looking at her. Non-Italian. His hands halfway inside his bag, looking for something.

In that split second the whole world seemed to fall into place. It was *him*. The one and only, the one she knew she could melt with. She just knew, not knowing where that knowledge came from.

He knew and she knew.

The world stood still, and noise and madness fell apart.

It was quiet.

Their eyes met and connected them to their infinite souls.

The meeting was absolute.

Seconds passed but it felt as if eternity entered Roma Termini.

Her friend came back.

Katrin answered.

Lost in the sense of being in an infinite space with another being.

She looked back.

His eyes were gone.

"I need something to eat".

"Yes let's go and get a baguette and think about our options".

"I don't' want to stay here".

"Me neither" she said.

"Did you see that?"

"What?"

"The guys from yesterday?"

"Noooo, you have got to be kidding! Shit you're right; it's them, what is happening? Look down, look away, I don't want them to see us".

"I think it's too late"… her friend smiled to her, as they could see the three guys had seen them, and were heading towards them".

She felt really uncomfortable, and embarrassed, she had left the train without saying goodbye – not her style.

He was good looking – they all were.

"Hi again".

They all looked really tired.

"Hi".

"So, what happened to Florence?"… they smiled at them in a cheeky way.

"Couldn't stay there without a tent".

"So where are you going now?"

They were silent.

They didn't know.

"You could come with us to Greece, the train is leaving for Brindisi in 2 hours?"

It was not the guy she had kissed.

He was more quiet.

They were looking at each other.

"Let's think about it. Where can we find you?"

"Track 16".

They went to buy a baguette. So many people, she felt dirty. Tired of Italy already. She swore that she would never be back. She looked around at all the people, the trains, the food. She decided that she hated it all. She hated Italy. All apart from the special eyes.

"I know you don't like that guy, but they are sweet, and you don't have to kiss him again. I want to go, and I don't know where else we should go. Do you? I mean, I feel safe with the guys, they protect us from the Italians".

"I agree, let's go"

"I can't wait to get out of here".

"Me too".

"God, I'm not coming back, that's for sure. I don't like to go with the guys, but I don't like it here either. What is it with this guy. Why did I even kiss him? I got drunk, I suppose. Boy what a mess and we have just begun our travels. And the other man, I'll never forget that look. God please bring him to me again".

They went to track 16.

She glanced at the arches of the ceiling… *"Roma Termini, I will never see you again, I swear".*

The train departed.

You can swear that you never will, but it's very hard to shut up the voice of your soul.

More than 20 years later she was back.

"Fuck, where did I put the ticket? What freaking chaos this is".

He was sweating a lot, looked down into his backpack, what a mess. He was not really known for having things in order. Or for having a sense of direction for that matter.

He relied on the others. They knew that.

And he knew that he was a real pain in the ass sometimes, but even though he was totally disorganized most of the time; he always knew what he wanted.

That frustrated people.

They wanted him to follow them, now that they were organizing the mess he made, but he didn't.

He was connected to a higher voice in life.

He knew he was different from others. He cared about people but he didn't care about what they said. He tried to please others for a while, but in the end he always did it his way anyway.

"Where is that damn ticket, come on….. sense it now. You know it's here, damn it's hot… the train is leaving soon, and I just want to get out of this Roma Termini or what ever it's called".

His younger brother and their two friends, where looking at him now. Clearly annoyed.

"Come on Michael, don't give us this crap, you have got to get your stuff together. I mean we need to catch the train. I want to go home".

They only had 45 minutes to get the train back up north.
They had to reach their hometown again.
Copenhagen.

"I know", he snapped back.

"Can't you just go and get some food and drinks for the trip, I'll find it then".

"Sure".

"Can't they just shut up, they do it every time and they know how I am. They know I'm disorganized… shit, where is that thing".

Beads of sweat were running down his dark brown hair. He didn't look that Scandinavian. It was like he was born in the wrong country, wrong place... He felt so wrong and at the same time he felt like he was so right, it was just the others that didn't get it. He had a lot of energy and he just wanted to use it. He saw patterns in life that others didn't. He saw the opportunities. He didn't care about all the right stuff... Yet he was longing for someone to understand that part of his soul, which no one seemed to grasp.

He pushed away the thought. The shorts were sticking to his ass and climbing up, so he had to pull them down.

He glanced out.

He saw the trains, the shops, the people and the mess.

Suddenly the feeling of slow motion entered his consciousness.

That was when he saw *her*.

She was standing all-alone, waiting for someone.

She looked a bit resigned.

He stopped.

Observed her features. Her cheekbones were very marked. Soft lips. Strong eyes.

She looked up, glancing out.

She was wearing a red tank top that softly showed of her beautiful rounded breasts. Her shorts were denim cut-offs.

His heart stopped, his breathing stopped. He felt that time stood still. It was not just her beauty. It was something different... Like she was the female version of him. How could he sense that from here?

How could he sense that it was just *her*?

He couldn't take his eyes of her.

Katrin saw him; they looked into each other eyes. It felt like he had known her for years, the best ever, the best moment ever. He knew at that very second that she would understand. Understand that part of him, which no one else did.

Lars shouted

"What's up Michael? Did you find it?"

He was confused, what? How?... his eyes left hers.

"No, I forgot… I mean, I know, but see, it's her".
"What do you mean by that? Michael, what happened, did you get hit by a train?"

They were laughing… He could hear them in the background.
He looked up again and she was gone…

"Where are you? How could I let it happen? Oh God! She was there, I know. It was her. *And now she is gone. DAMN!!!!"*

His brother and their two friends, looked at him.

"What happened?"
"I saw her".
"What do you mean by that?"
"The woman".
"Stop it now, there are so many beautiful women out there".

They were cracking up with really bad jokes.
He knew it was time to shut up. They would never understand… They moved on. The train was about to part.

Copenhagen was calling.

He looked back… maybe he could see her. Would he run if he did?

No sight of her.

He was heading north.
She was heading south.
They were from the same country.
Was it a love meant to be?
And if!
Then… When?

THREE

On Her Way

She stood at the self service check-in counter at the airport. Katrin was eager to go, excited, feeling it was going to be the trip of her life. No response. It must be wrong. She had just bought the ticket yesterday – the second one. She had already booked one ticket to Venice, months ago, and then yesterday, in a minute, everything had changed.

An email had arrived announcing that an extra day had been added to the seminar.

"I have to go, this is amazing, and I will buy another ticket, no matter what the cost."

She had been really excited when she was typing the digits on the visa card, so it had been done in a second. Then began hurriedly finishing off the last bit of work so she could go home and pack for the trip.

"Ahh Venice, what will you bring to me? How much adventure will you bring? How much wisdom will you reveal?"

Katrin had seen the poster for this seminar while she was attending another seminar. She had been checking it out on the website regularly, like a secret forbidden lover. Every time she looked at it, it felt like it screamed to her, take me, come to me, I need you here. It was like a spotlight was on it, wanting to draw her into a new scene in life.

No question about it, she was adventurous and she loved meeting new people, travels, education, spirits, joy and love. But the pain inside her soul was haunting her, and she would do anything in the world to meet the right people who were able to help her, release that pain, face it, transform it. She couldn't fathom why the seminar had such an appeal to her, although often the things she had done in life had not made any sense right away anyway, yet with this she just knew she had to attend.

Damn! She had tried three times now and the machine still said that she was not onboard. What's wrong? Assistance was coming.

"Do you have a ticket?"

"Yes she said – I booked it yesterday, here it is." She was fumbling with the papers and there it was, the ticket!

"It's not today, the ticket is not for today"

She looked at her "What are you saying?"

"It's says here, it's for tomorrow".

She was looking at the paper, not believing what she saw.

"But I already have a ticket for tomorrow" "It can't be right!"

The assistance looked at her with an understanding smile.

"Over there you can get another ticket". She pointed at another counter.

"Thanks!" and she was already on the run.

Katrin got desperate, looking at the big clock in the departure terminal. She had gone from having lots of time to nothing and now she was without a ticket. She wanted to go, she wanted to go today, she had to. Her heart was beating fast; she was looking at the clock again, and again... running now. Would she be able to get a new ticket?

She was speaking in a high, thin voice desperate to go, desperate to get the ticket. There was not much time. The lady was patient, doing her best to get the cheapest fare for her. She got one... laughing to herself... she now had three tickets to Venice and one of them was for right now. Within 45 minutes the plane would leave Denmark, taking her away to Venice. She started to relax.

"What is it with this trip? Why is it so important that it feels like life or death? Like I would die, if I couldn't have gone. It feels so strong, this trip, which is waiting for me. I know that when I feel this stubbornness inside me, I just have to go. I know it's important. A puzzle in my soul is to be shown a very important piece.

It's also a bit funny, as if the universe or God is testing me, wanting me to feel how much I really want this".

Katrin was walking with her suitcase, thinking about what had happened in the past ½ hour. She was reflecting. She was always reflecting on the moments in life. Especially when the voice of the soul was this strong. When her soul wanted her to go somewhere in life, she could try to resist it, but she knew in the end she would always go, when her soul told her so. Everyone had always told her, that she had so much courage, but she had really never had any choice whether or not to follow her heart. She had always envied people who were able to shut down that inner voice of their heart because she was convinced, that they did not suffer as much inner pain as she did.

She was leaning back in the seat feeling the comfort of the chair while looking out of the little window into the gray outside.

"It has been the worst spring ever. First a long cold winter and then a rainy spring. I'm so looking forward to go to Italy".

The plane pushed back, she loved the takeoff from Denmark.

The wheels were moving, the plane jumping a bit over the bumps on the ground, the engine was making more noise and she took a deep breath. Now the plane was still. And then suddenly the engines starting to move really fast, the feeling of the steel's tension was in her seat.

"Freeeedoooommmm……. I love it! I love leaving Denmark. Every time, this is the best part, when the wheels sets off".

At the airport, the feeling of hot stickiness touching her skin made her so happy. Katrin was crazy about the heat. Her body had just waited all winter long and the awful spring to meet the sun. And now she was here with the buzz of the taxis, the warm wind and Italian words flying around. She felt so relaxed now that she had arrived – she just needed to go to the hotel outside Venice.

"Ciao, is this my taxi?"

"Yes, it is. We are just waiting for a couple of other people, then we will leave".

Three other people joined the taxi and it left. She was looking out the windows as the car drove through the Italian landscape. She hadn't been in Italy since she was 18 years old and she had hated it. She had actually sworn, that she would never go back to this place.

"Maybe you can't swear that you won't do things, here I am back in the country I thought I never would go back to, and it just feels so right".

She was listing to the conversation of the three other passengers. It was quite amusing hearing them talk about the conference they were going to attend. They were all in the game, the game of being be the cleverest one, the most important one. Who was going to speak at the conference, who knew the most people and so on. She could tell that it was a conference on a certain subject. They were naming a lot of key speakers. Katrin tried to grasp the subject, geography… maybe. Ah, she wasn't sure. She thought it was funny though and she was smiling inside, because every time there was a pause, you could just feel the inner tension in all of them. Not really knowing what to say, and then again talking a lot, in an attempt to sound very excited. But mostly she could hear the tension leave them as soon as they didn't have to sit in silence. They got out of the taxi in a small Italian town graced with amazing houses, the old Italian classic feeling. It was now just her and the taxi driver. Soon they were near her destination.

She arrived at the hotel, tired, the feeling of having completed a long journey filled her body. She was lying down on her bed, exhausted, happy and tired. She had made it. She took a shower and a nap. Soon it would be time for dinner.

"Where would you like to sit, alone or with the others?"
"Alone?"
"Okay mam, this way please".

"Why is he saying that? Does he know that I'm here for the seminar? Probably. But that means that the others are here. Where are they?"

Karin's eyes glanced out into the restaurant, looking to see if she could spot the teacher of the seminar, and just as the waiter showed her to her table, she saw him and a whole table full of people.

"Those must be all the other participants for the seminar starting tomorrow".

She glanced at the table just to make sure that she was right, and at that moment a man with a very straight posture, beamed out and their eyes met. This was more than merely just noticing someone, it was a look that was so intense that she felt a burn in her soul. It was amazing that one look felt as if she had encountered something very important, something that added to the puzzle of her soul. It was not the same experience as the guy on the train station in Rome. Suddenly she was thinking about him again. Even though it was 20 years ago, he still was in her heart. She just knew that some day, that would fall into place…

"I wish that I had chosen to sit with the others, now it's a bit late. They look like they are having so much fun at the other table.
Anyway it's also nice just to sit here and read. I feel quite tired. I don't have to be so social, that's quite nice too".

Katrin left the restaurant and went to the reception area. She asked where the seminar would be held in the morning. The receptionist said that this guy would know as she was pointing at the teacher who had suddenly appeared in the reception hall. She walked towards him.

"Hi, I'm going to attend the seminar tomorrow".
"Hi, nice to met you, where are you from?"
"I'm from Denmark".
"Nice".
"Do you know where the seminar will take place tomorrow?"
"No, I don't know, but the guys at the table know, ask them".
"Thanks! I'll see you tomorrow".
"Yes, good night".
"Good night".

She walked back into the restaurant and straight to the table where all the Italians were sitting. She said "Ciao" and walked around the table, greeting everyone.

Two guys who were in charge of the seminar (she later found out), said that she should sit down for a bit and she did. Katrin was talking a bit, completely forgetting that the guy whose eyes she had met earlier on was just sitting at the table.

They asked where she was from, how many seminars she had done. She was tired, so she politely turned down the offer for a glass of wine, and left the table to get herself ready for the next day; the first day of the seminar.

She was excited and tired. The energy at the table had been good and she felt that it was going to be a fantastic seminar. As she was closing her eyes her mind raced through all the events of the day. It felt like a week had been crammed into only one day.

Life was strange, now she was here. In Italy… Who would have thought that?

Katrin woke up early. She was generally not sleeping that well. Outside on the balcony, her naked skin absorbed the heat of the morning as she watched the sun rising. Waking up and already feeling the warmness in the air was amazing. The quietness of the still sleepy hotel filled the air.

She sat there for a while just reflecting on life before she put on her running clothes and went for a run in the gym. After the morning exercise, she collected her breakfast on a tray and went back upstairs to her hotel room: she was not in the mood to meet anyone from the seminar.

She was about to walk down the stairs to the seminar room when she walked by some people who were about to take the lift.

"Want to come?" a guy asked.
"No".

The door closed and she barely saw the woman, as a shadow, when the doors closed. The Italian woman from Northern Ireland. She was here… Rosa.

"All these small hidden links in life, unfolding so beautifully. Or maybe I'm putting too much into this, but then again… It feels like it's an important sign showing me, that I'm on the right track".

She walked into the seminar room; the coolness in the air from the air conditioning fan surprised her. She had wanted the heat. She then quickly said hi to the coordinator and got checked-in before she found a chair in the front row.

It was really exciting to be here and it was a very small seminar. She felt a happiness just being here, just hearing the Italians talking to each other made her happy. There was an excitement in the air, the Italians sounded so happy to see each other and it felt like she had joined a big family.

"I'm looking back, if I just glance for a second I can see them. I'm sure that it's those eyes I saw yesterday at the dinner… yes they are there, just behind me…"

"You're turn".
"Me?"
"Yes, hop up".
"Okay".

She was nervous, lying down on the treatment table, as the teacher was about to undertake the session. The whole Italian group were there just looking at her.

Then he began talking for a long time. She was just lying there; waiting for the treatment to take place… nothing… instead they broke for coffee and tea.

Then, finally the treatment session was experienced. Katrin hadn't quite known what to expect, maybe that the heaven would fall down on her? Maybe that the pain of her inner soul would have suddenly disappeared? She knew that was not why she was there, but secretly it was what she had hoped for. Something in the bigger picture of her life was unfolding…

The day went on and she was so happy to be here. During lunch the first day, the energy around the table was very much alive; everyone was so open, so chatty and so warm. She was overwhelmed with all this joy, it was amazing and in a matter of seconds she fell in love with the whole group around the table. They were asking questions, who? How? Why? Where? It was like having an instant family.

They were all smiling and laughing as she began learning new Italian words, pepe, sale, olio.

Every time, she had a minute she walked outside of the hotel with a cup of tea to just inhale the sun. It was so amazing, feeling the heat, just sitting and relaxing, filling up her body with the sun's rays. It had been too long now, with no sun. The sun was magical.

"I'm heartened something is really moving here. I feel touched, like I've found a home with them. It does something to me Italy: the people, the language, the ambience. I feel that a part of me is relaxing for the first time since I had messed up my soul…., something is right here, something is to be healed, deep within".

Katrin had cried at one point in the class, the tears slowly running down her cheek. He had moved her, the teacher. Something he had said had touched her, and the secret pain she held within. The unspeakable pain she could not tell anyone about.

He later asked her, what it was that touched her. And she had shared it with him. He had understood. He knew someone else who had also created a pain in her soul. He said that he could get her number. But she had said no for she was afraid that further discussion would only make things worse.

Throughout the seminar their eyes would frequently really connect. The magic eyes from the first day. It was as if their eyes knew something that they didn't.

They talked some, not much.

It was as if he popped up all the time.

She was alone in a cafe far away from the hotel. Warm coffee, feet up. He passed her. Stopped. Strange, like he just knew where she was. Would she exchange some sessions when she came home? Sure…

A friendship began.
Luca and Katrin.

They talked later, just a little.
Then they said goodbye.

Katrin went home with a new family, and Italy in her heart. Knowing she had found an energy for healing.

It was the energy of a whole country. Some people living 2000 kilometers away.

Life had to show some magic. She knew she had to go back. But how and when?

The future was yet to be written in the theater play she was calling life.

FOUR

The Angel Boy Is Born

The angel boy was born at home in the early spring. The joy of the newborn boy was immense, in a way that only the Italians knew how to master to perfection. Expressing their emotions in the most outstanding way. There was wine, bread, cheese, pasta, words flying around, joy, kisses, laughter, the celebration of a new soul – it was a joyful day. The family had grown from four to five.

The mother's heart was fully embracing the new soul as he laid in her arms. She knew that he was different; it was easy to tell. She could feel his soul, his heart and his energy. He was special. His face was different too; you could see it, with your naked eyes. He had some physical deficiencies.

They were in shock, it was not expected. The reactions could have been one of many. Either you embrace it or you fight it.

They did the first. It was instant.

The families' hearts were open, as the sunshine boy landed in the small village Pitigliano, in the middle of Tuscany.

This is a very special village. The first written words are from 1061 and the village is built with huge rocks taken from part of the cliffs in the landscape. Driving up to Pitigliano and seeing it from a distance is breathtaking. It's so impressive to see the enormous stone buildings on the cliffs, with rocks that are up to 10 meters long. The village people have made a parking space just opposite the town, from where you are able to gaze over the village as you are approaching.

Giovanni, the local wine merchant, has opened a small shop there, just on that spot, surrounded by big trees, so you can have a glass of wine in the shade, and also buy some of the fine wines when you're going home.

Giovanni was a very close friend to the Sebastino family. It often felt like he was an uncle to the three boys although he was not a blood relation. Giovanni means "a gift from God" and he truly was a gift from God to the family.

He was a man with a loud laughter, great wisdom and a heart of gold. In his presence you could feel his deep silent knowing and understanding of people's deepest thoughts and actions. The special way he knew the grapes of the wines he was selling. Where the grapes had been hanging, who had showed the grapes their love whilst growing in the Italian sun. His perception around grapes and wine was very similar to the way he knew people. He knew the soul of the wine, the heart of the wine. He knew the souls and hearts of people...

Giovanni was rushing to the house. Francesca, his wife, had called him from the home of the Sebastino family. The boy had arrived, they had know it for some time. Now he was here. They sounded happy, but he also knew that something was wrong. He glanced up, half running, half walking "ciao" he said "ciao, ciao" – he knew many people in the town. Many "ciaos" were expressed.

Sebastino's house was just outside the village, on the right, it stood there orange and red under a big tree with a view from the house that was spectacular. One could see the town a bit up on the left, the rocks on the cliffs and the valley just in the front. It was warm, even for a spring day. Giovanni walked through the garden gate as the dog and his wife came out to greet him. He could see her joy, but also a sorrow in her face.

"He's here".

He was waiting for her to tell him more.
She was nervous, he could tell, her eyes were wet and she was looking around, talking a lot about this and that. Her arms and hands all over the place. He gently took her right hand, and with all his silence soothed her to coax the words from her lips.

"The boy… the angel boy… he has some physical deficiencies, but he is so beautiful, so adorable, he is big and chubby…"

She was laughing, half crying, the tears were running down her cheek, smiling… He took her in his arms and held her for a very long time. He was just there, in silence, feeling her body jumping a little, while the tears and the sorrow were flowing. Then she took a deep breath and he could feel her body relaxing… he released his arms, held her face gently with both hands, looked her deep in the eyes and said:

"It doesn't matter… I bet he is special" – he smiled warmly at her.

"Yes, very, you should see his eyes, they have stars".

"I can't wait to see him".

They walked into the house. Straight into the huge open kitchen with the big table in the middle of the room full of food and wine – the ambience was warm and cheerful "chin chin", people were laughing, celebrating the new soul that had arrived. The fireplace was lit, even though it was a hot day outside, the house could still be cold.

In the middle of the chaos of people he saw her, Celia, the mother of the angel boy on the sofa holding her baby son. Giovanni glanced at her, she looked tired, but my God was she beautiful! Looking at her watching her new son so closely, smiling, tears running down her cheeks… he was silent. Then she looked up and their eyes met, she smiled, he smiled back…

Her eyes said "Come and see"…

He walked over to her, sat gently on the sofa beside her and looked at her, then at the boy… he was sleeping. He just knew in that moment that he was something special, whether or not he had some physical deficiencies; he had something to teach us all. He was a true gift from God. And Giovanni felt in that moment that he had made a special bond with the angel boy, one that could never be broken.

"I know he is not…"

"But my Goodness, he is…"

The words came fumbling out of her… she didn't need to say anything, he already knew.

Silently they sat, watching him, sensing him, he was awake now, something in his eyes, Francesca was right, they were like stars lighting up.

"He is wise".
She looked up and smiled "Yes, very".
"But how?"
"He is clearly disabled".
"That doesn't mean that he is not wise" he said – "Don't let the wrapping confuse you, you know how lucky you are, you're blessed with an amazing soul, amazing heart. Look at him... I know you can see, it's all you need".

"I know, I know", her tears were running now.
"It's just, but can I? I'm scared" her voice was low.
"If anyone can take care of him Celia, it's you. I know you can, and we're all here, you're not alone".

He wrapped his left arm around her and held her, until he felt her body relaxed. Her sister came and took the angel boy out of her hands.

"Rest my dear".

Celia smiled and laid down.

"I will".

Giovanni looked up and saw that the older brothers where there, they were quite older than the angel boy, seven and nine years. They smiled at him, he spread his arms, they ran to him, and he squeezed them so hard, laughing out loud and they laughed with him. Boy, did he love those boys.

He and Francesca did not have the fortune to create life.

He hugged and hugged them, all becoming one and he told them:

"Bellissimo… You're so lucky that you received such a beautiful brother".

He felt the boy's unease with the abnormal traits of their baby brother… hence he repeated again and again how lucky they were and how very special they were having received such a blessing of a special brother. This was Giovanni's greatest gift to the Sebastino's, he could make everything easier, and he could make the sun shine even brighter than it was.

The boys smiled. Celia looked at her husband Fabio, they smiled, looked at their three boys, they knew that even if the situation was not the way they had asked for, they were blessed, so blessed.

Needless to say, his name became Angelo. But in a way he was just always the angel boy.

Angel boy had found his spot in the world. He was here.

He was growing up, always doing things with a twist, dancing, laughing and spreading joy in the family, more that you could ever have imagined.

He always did things, that were a bit out of place, but he did it in such a way that, it only added to the whole. It was only when he got angry or confused when the situation became really up tight, that he would scream.

The kitchen, the heart of the house, this is where he was, with his mother, always.

When he was a toddler, he was running around her legs, playing around while she was cooking. He went to the market with her. He loved it. He was running around, watching and touching all the vegetables, looking at the meats, the nuts and the fish. He loved meeting people, it was magic to him. The village loved him. All of them called him "Angel boy, Angel boy" when he was coming, they wanted to give him sweets. He was happy, running around all the people, loving him. He was full by the time they were walking home. He had eaten up so much love.

Angelo was intelligent, determined and extremely stubborn. Whenever he wanted something, it had to be right here and now.

And he was noisy, indeed. But in Italy who really cares? The louder the better.

The brothers absolutely adored Angel boy.

The middle brother, Luca, was a very sensitive boy and he felt sorry for his brother at times. But the love between them was special. Very special. Angelo loved to climb up in his lap, tucking in, feeling so safe in his arms.

The Angel boy adored his older brothers; he thought they were the coolest guys in the world.

Luca was popular even if he was a silent and a private boy. He had a magnetic energy, people were drawn to him, but often because they wanted to protect him and try to fill in the gap of the never ending sadness there was hanging around him. He would let people in close for a while, but then like a turtle, retreat back into his shell.

The world overwhelmed him at times.

He loved being in his room alone, he loved writing about the life he saw unfolding in front of him. He often covered it up in wild scenarios, so as to make it more fun. He got into his own world and stayed there. Luca would sit there for hours and only when the restlessness captured his body did he go out into the kitchen to be with his mom and his brothers.

Angelo saw him coming out of the room and ran over to him. He smiled like no one could, lifting his arms.

Luca lifted up his brother and watched him, he held him close. He smiled, the Angel boy was the sun, he was the moon. He had become the life energy that Luca needed.

Angel boy loved many things and took great delight in talking about how much he loved them. He loved people, food, life – he could not get enough. One of his favorite moments was always when they visited Giovanni, he could stay there for hours. Giovanni always let him help him. He would stand on a chair by the till in the shop and greet people coming in for wine. He would talk non-stop, always making the customers laugh and spreading sunshine in the shop.

He was the sun.

These were the moments when Celia got to have a break.

In the evenings he would tuck in bed with his brother and they would sing the day goodbye, and welcome the night. He loved when his brother started to read "Buonanotte giraffa" to him.

They had a place in his room, lots of blankets and cushions, stars hanging down.

The light was just enough to read by.

Angel boy laughed every time at the same place in the book, when in the story the giraffe was dangling his legs on the zebra's shoulder.

He was special.
Angel boy.
Living a normal life.
Spreading joy.
Spreading love.
Knowing what he wanted.
And his heart.
Was of gold.
The purest.
So pure that the gift of it,
Would take it much further,
Than you could ever;
Imagine

FIVE

The Pain Of Life

She was always watching people. Looking at them, wondering why they did the things they did. It seemed like they had been born with some kind of formula to life. One that she had not been given.

It felt like only the ones with the formula were invited to the real party of life.

How did she have right to be here?

Katrin often felt, that she didn't have the right to exist.

No party to go to.

And what kind of party would she want to go to?

She knew that a lot more children like her would be born into this world.

People didn't seem to understand them.

She liked the truth.

Other people didn't.

They ran.

They lied to others, but mostly to themselves.

She could smell it.
Sense it.
Miles away.
She tried to be like them.
Tried to lie, but she couldn't.
It made her sick.
Physically.
Emotionally.
She soul was in pain.
She wanted to be clean.
Clean in every sense.

She hadn't known how different she was from other people in sensing the world beyond until she became a grown up.
So much repair had to be done.
She cried a lot, it helped her shut the world off.
Water.
Cheeks.
Tears were her protection.
People thought she was sad.
Mostly she was angry.
Scared.

She had many thoughts, when she was a little girl, about getting away from this world. It was too big and she was too scared.
She planned strategies.

"If I just stopped speaking, then I wouldn't have to deal with other people, I wouldn't have to express emotions. I could be free but then again, is that what I want to do with my life?"

She had been five.
She had wished she could stay like that forever.

Five became her lucky number.
Pure logic.

She felt that she had been given a secret map of roads in life, one in which people around her did not get nor see. She knew some shortcuts. But she just didn't want that gift. She wanted to be like all the others.

Then there was this…
She saw things.
She knew how things would be.
In a larger perspective.
Ahead of time.
She tried to avoid the information.
Tried not to listen to it.
It only made things worse.
Her heart was beating for one specific route in life. She knew it inside. She could feel it. She knew the way that was best for her. It was not the road taken by others.
But she had to follow it.
Follow that beating part of her.
The part, which held all the knowledge.
The heart.
She was fighting it a lot.
Afraid that if she followed it, she would expose herself.
That was bad.
She was different.
She knew.
Said weird stuff.
But it just came through.

Her pain… she had to follow her heart.

She didn't understand the world, but she really wanted to. She wanted to understand what it was all about. What was the meaning of life? What was the meaning of *her* life?

She tried to understand ordinary people in order to understand her. That didn't work, that made her feel even more odd.

She had been given this pain of life, she knew, and she was not happy about it. She was fighting it, yelling at it, screaming at it.

But only on the inside.

She had seen it coming.
She knew it.
Therapy.
That was going to be a way forward in her life.
She couldn't avoid it.
She was scared of it.
Not a lot of people did therapy
When she had begun.

But she had to look at it.
The pain.
The pain she had been given.

She had been told that she was going to do it the hard way. She didn't want to dope her soul.

"Why do they think it's good to become a pot with a lid? Then you have to live with the uncertainty that the lid can blow off... and then what? What would happen then?"

She just pictured an image of crap pouring out of her brain. Crap that had become even stickier over all the years, the brain and the soul had been doped.

She was looking for the truth, even if it hurt so damn hard
sometimes.
Even if she had to take full responsibility for all the crap.
She wanted to belong.
Meet the souls that she knew were out there.
They *were* there.
She just had to find them.
But she had to solve her inner puzzle.
The one that had been broken.
The puzzle of her soul.

She had to accept wherever her heart was going.
Easy, no.
Fun, no.
Teaching, yes.

She had found a new job.
She became a seeker.
Seeking her truth.
Seeking the love of life.
There was one catch.
You didn't earn.
You had to pay.
Still it would be money well spent.
She had no idea how to achieve it.
But she just had to.

They hadn't taught her to be a seeker in school;
This was just something driving her from within.
But she had a plan.
To not seek for long.
Just long enough to have the pain transformed.

"If I can just devote myself 100% to this, and do it honestly all the time, then it would be over much faster. I know, I can get there. I know that there is something beyond this pain. I know that I can fix it. I know that there is happiness created for me, somewhere out there".

She figured that, the bigger the leaps she could take, the quicker it would go. But it didn't.

She had set backs.

Big ones.

She got so annoyed.

It took time.

Time away from the real goal; to get it done.

Done as quickly as she could.

Katrin had been a seeker now for 13 years. Her definition of being a seeker was to find the key to the pain in her soul. Once found, her pain would vanish.

She was wrong.

It was only now it all had begun.

But really, when do things start and when do they end. Maybe never?

"I have read all the books, I know all the "right" spiritual stuff. But when you're in it, it's so much harder. It's so easy to write about it rather than experience it. But I still have to seek until I find the key to my pain."

She was looking back at all the years of pain.

From this man, the therapist, she could sense the very energy she had been looking for her whole life. She had found the key.

So what to do?

She couldn't hang around him for the rest of her life. She wanted the knowledge, that piece of energy she saw when she was in the same room as him. It was not romantic. It was practical; she had to get the information.

She had a plan.

From all the years of therapy, she had a knowing. She had learned projections, and how to look at them. She forced herself to look at them.

Damn she had been smart and clever.

It just hadn't worked, at all.

She had scratched a very deep groove in the river of her soul, and the result was a flood, running with such speed that no mind would have a chance to follow.

She was in the shit.

Free falling.

She could sense it.

She was falling apart.

But inside her there was a stubborn lion, which wouldn't give up. No matter how hard it was, no matter how dissolving she felt. No matter how lost she looked in the eyes of other people. She knew she could do it.

It became her inner secret. No one was to know. She felt that if she said it out loud, she would vanish completely; afraid of not being able to find herself again.

A new chapter had started and she had to follow the unknown path of life, the life that indeed was hers, and was written for her.

She just had to follow the clues, the senses and the visions that were given to her.

They were already present in her story of life. Just waiting for her to open them up.

She couldn't move quickly now.

She had to listen.

Listen to what was right for her.

At every given moment.

Often she came home from a walk and hadn't done what she had intended to do. Her body and her soul, wanted to do something different.

She didn't dare not listen.

The overwhelming rush of energy, the uncontrollable river was stronger than her.

She was full of fear.

People said it was a nice spiritual feeling.

She would rather sell it.

If she could sell or give it away for free, she would have been so joyful. But you can't sell your soul, it's yours and you have to deal with it.

She felt she had fucked-up her soul! But can you really fuck it up?

She was fighting herself, her own energy.

That made her worse.

There was no one around.

She just had to trust her strength and that what she had been shown in this energy was right, even though the pain was so overwhelming.

She had been shown how a man and a woman could be together. How they could melt into each other.

How to be pure love…

She was in the middle of her deepest pain, and had only one way to go.

SIX

The Angel Boy Is Growing

"Belloooooooo... Angeloooooo" Celia was calling Angelo.

Normally you could hear him miles away, even if they were at the market with all its noise, she could always hear and sense him.

But now it was completely silent.

"Angeloooo, where are you my darling? – Mi Amore"

She was smiling and laughing a bit to herself.

Boy had life changed since Angel boy had arrived in the family?

Everything had changed, not that she would complain in any way, but he demanded people to be present. Celia would get exhausted at times, but he also brought an unlimited amount of joy and liveliness into the house.

She had stopped working when he arrived; she and Fabio had made that decision together.

She had no doubt whatsoever; with his arrival it felt like a part of her life had in some how fallen into place.

She had thought about that a lot. How could it be that an inner peace had come to her, when he had arrived? Like her soul had known, that he was to come and that her life was meant to unfold like this. How could such a challenging child still bring so much peace with him?

Over the years she often remembered Giovanni's words whenever she felt in doubt. *"If there is anyone who can do it, then it is you Celia"*… The words comforted her when she felt tired.

Her thoughts were wandering; she thought of Giovanni and she smiled to herself.

"Belloooooo, Bello, Bello, where are you? I can't find you." He did this a lot. He loved it. He loved hiding from her. Normally it was the same places he would go to. Just next to the fireplace, and in his brother's room and sometimes under their bed. But this time she couldn't find him. It was a sunny day, his birthday, so she knew he was especially excited. Five years…

She began to sing "Se sei Felice", he loved that song. She could hear him starting to giggle, he was so excited now and she knew that. He had so much joy in his body and he loved when they were playing.

"Bellooooo"… She started dancing and singing, clapping her hands. Suddenly he jumped out of a cupboard and he laughed and laughed and laughed… he was running around in his underwear and singing with his mother.

She picked him up, smiled at him.

"Belloooo you need to put your clothes on. You know how I love to play games with you, but we're having your birthday party in two hours and I need to cook. I can't play anymore. Okay?"

"Okay Mama".

He was laughing and kissing her all over her face, then in a split second he wrestled out of her arms and ran upstairs to his brothers.

She smiled to herself as she went into the kitchen. Time to cook.

Giovanni found Angelo under a tree in the garden. He could see that he was sitting under his favorite "secret" tree. It was way back in the garden. He knew that Celia was watching him. You could easily see the tree from the kitchen window. He knew Angelo and his Mama had an agreement that if he wanted to be alone, he could sit under his "secret" tree. Everyone knew that it was Angelo's tree, but to Angelo it was his secret.

Giovanni was walking with quiet and strong steps. He didn't want to scare Angelo, he knew that when he was sitting here, it was because he was reflecting.

This boy was special.

He was full of humbleness and love for this five year-old boy. His heart became warm when looking at him.

He sat quietly on a stone, watching him.

He knew Celia was watching him.

Just waiting.

Waiting for him to move.

He knew it could take some time.

Celia had called; she knew that when he was in this mood only Luca and Giovanni could reach him.

Often she could too, but once in a while, mama was no good.

Luca was in school.

Giovanni had come immediately.

Over the years Angelo had become a little bit more aware of the ways he stood out. It was still early on, but still…

All of them took it seriously.

To support him.

Support his pain.

Even if he was Mr. Sunshine.

They all respected his new awareness of not being as the others.

Luca and Angelo had a also a very special bond. Luca seemed to be able to reach Angelo without words. It was not the same with Giuseppe, his other brother, not that they didn't love each other but Luca just knew by heart that Angelo did not require the need to exchange any words. But Luca was in school.

Today Angelo had been so sad, he had ran out into the garden. She knew he respected her to sit under the tree and not leave the ground. But she had been concerned.

Giovanni had taken a deep breath.

"I know you're there Giovanni, I don't want to talk to you".
"I know, it's okay, I'm just sitting here".

They sat in silence, but Giovanni knew better, he knew that Angelo would begin to speak soon. He closed his eyes, felt the sun and smiled.

"I hate this".
"What do you hate?"
"I hate this life".
"Why, my dear?"
"I don't like that I'm different".
"I know my dear. But you know what?"
"No".

Angelo turned his face around; Giovanni could see the tears that had been running down his cheeks.

"God made you special, only because he knew you could do it. Only because he knew that you were so blessed within you. Not many people have that ability. Did you know that?"
"No…"

Angelo had come over to him and sat down on his lap. Squeezing himself into Giovanni. Giovanni had his arms around him.

"I want ice cream".

Giovanni laughed out loud and took Angelo in his arms.

"Then we'll go for ice cream", and they both laughed together.

Angelo had a very special gift.
He could shift from low to high in a split second.

It was Giovanni's weekly day, well it was also Francesca's, but he loved it the most. They both knew that.
Silently.

This one day a week Angelo stayed with Giovanni and Francesca.

They did the same every time.

First ice cream.

Then to the wine-shop, where Angelo would run around playing that he was helping with the till. He was always talking and laughing up a storm.

The whole town simply loved him. He was chit chatting with everyone.

His remarks came totally uncensored from the heart.

After that, they always walked home to Giovanni and Francesca's, buying food and drinks for the evening on the way.

Angelo would always get a lollipop.

Once they got home, they sat down on the veranda where Giovanni got a coffee and Angelo some juice.

They always had plenty of time. No rush. Angelo loved that. Just to be.

They watched a bit of TV and then Giovanni began to cook.

They had pasta, different ones.

After that, they read and went to bed.

Giovanni and Angelo had a very special connection.

Everyone knew.

It was nearly lunchtime and they were about to go pick up his brothers from school.

Angelo loved it.

He was running around, talking, hugging his mother and kissing her. Singing, clapping, dancing…

She locked the door.

He ran; he knew the way.

The school was close.

He was waiting by the school door.
All the friends were coming out.
"Ciao Angelo"
"Ciao",
"Ciao",
"Ciao."

All of Luca and Giuseppe's friends where saying ciao. They adored him.

Angelo was so excited, so happy. He wanted to hug them.
Some did.
Some didn't.
Luca and Giuseppe came out.

They grabbed him, and hugged him really hard... Laughing.

"Come Angelo, run."

They ran.
Celia watched the boys. Damn they were good brothers. She was so very proud of them, and felt so blessed that the sensitive Luca and vigorous Giuseppe were there.
She couldn't ask for more.

They ran over the square, they knew their way.
Passed the small drinking fountain, where everyday they took a sip of water.
She walked gracefully behind them. Smiling to all the people that she knew.

Today Fabio was at home for lunch.
He travelled a lot.

It was okay.
He was a good husband.

The boys knew nothing.
No one knew.
She felt lonely.
She was hiding it.

"Quiet boys, quiet."

They could get so loud sometimes.
It was difficult to get really angry with them.
They were just so joyful.

"Come here, sit down".

They sat down at the table.
When Fabio was home he did the blessing.

"Thank you God, blessed we are, for this food and for our family, buon appetito."

The silence ended and the talk began.
The noise of the Sebatinio's filled the house.

"Why am I so different God? Why have you chosen me to be so different? I know a part of me just feels so wrong in this body. I can see that all the others are here to live an ordinary life. What about me? I can't get a wife; I can't get a job...like a real one. I know I can stay here with Giovanni, but still, why? Why? Why? Why me?..."

Angelo had just turned 18; he was in a way an adult,
Yet, he would never really be one.

He was sitting under his "secret tree".
He was really sad.
He was in love with a girl.
He knew he could never have her.
He fell in love so easily.
Always.
Not just girls.
Life.
He showed his happiness to the world.
Sometimes he felt like a turtle.
Suddenly he had to withdraw.
Luca knew him so well, when he was in this state of emotions.

Luca came.

"What's up my brother?"

He sat down and put his arm around him.

"I love her".

Luca held his breath.

"I know, I can't have her, but I love her".

He was crying now.

Luca had been here before. He knew he couldn't' do anything for him other than stay and hold him, just be there.

He knew his pain. He could understand. He felt sorry for him.

He loved him so much.

It hurt him to see his brother in this pain.

"I know my brother, I know it's hard for you".

Angelo sat with his face in his lap.

Luca held his head with his hand.

"Love is many things my brother".

"Yes, but you know there is a difference between you and me. I can't get what you can".

"I know."

"Come let's have a walk. Let's go to Giovanni and surprise him, I think that would be fun. We can go to his bar and get some juice…. Hear some music. What do you think?"

"YEEESSSS, I love".

Luca smiled. The most beautiful quality about his brother was that he always managed to bring out the sun. To see life from a completely different angle.

He didn't linger.

He knew his sorrow.

But there was so little he could do.

He could be there.

And he was; as much as possible.

He was not home that much more.

He studied at Sienna's university.

Not so far away from home. But still, he was not around everyday.

He went inside. Hugged his beloved mama.

"I'm going for a walk with Angelo".
"Grazie, Bello, so nice to have you home".
"I know Mama".

He took an apple, gave a wink with his eye and took a bite.

God she missed him being here at home. But she knew that he had to do what he had to do.

She was alone more than ever.

With only Angelo at home now.

Time had passed so quickly.

He could never leave the house for good, like the two others.

She knew.

He knew.

They shared that pain.

They shared that joy.

Angelo had two big wishes in life: to have a job and a girlfriend.

He was very stubborn about this and nothing anyone could say would change his mind.

Celia didn't know what to do about it. How could she help it along?

The girlfriend was a hard task.

Not so sure about that one.

But the other one... hmmmm.

The whole town loved Angelo.

It was very special and very precious.

She went to see Giovanni.

"Ciao my friend".
"Ciao Cara Celia, how are you?"

She smiled, quietly.
They talked.
She asked.
He said yes.
Angelo had a job.
It was perfect.
Angelo would be so happy.
They agreed.
That Giovanni would ask him.
It was only a few hours a day:
In the shop and in the bar.
Small tasks. But he would get paid.

They had built a little room outside the house.
Here he lived:
On his own.
But still at home.
Life felt settled for him.

He was a party boy, loved dancing and talking in the bar.
He knew a lot.
    He was a blessed boy.
    Had so many around him.
    Who loved him.
    Even if he had been born with differences.
    They drank.
    They sang.
    They hugged.

They talk.

They laughed.

It was a normal day in Pitigliano.

The sun left the landscape only to start breathing the next day.

As we all do.

Until we have to go…

SEVEN

England... The Hotel

Katrin had packed her bag; she was on her way again.

It was summer.

She was wearing a yellow skirt; a low buttoned silk shirt, and the lace of her bra visible to the naked eye.

She was in very good time.

Had checked her ticket several times.

"It's okay.

It's the right date.

I'm going to get a cup of coffee. I'm so looking forward to this trip. Can't wait to get out again, and see what there is to learn this time. I don't even have a clue about what we're going to learn".

The ticket said Birmingham, England.

She had never been.

Small airplane.

She was boarding.

Took her book, leaned back.

This time she felt light in her seat.

The airplane pulled out.

The man next to her was new in her life.

What she didn't know was, that in the future he would become a very important teacher in life.

They had talked about love and the greater life.

She had briefly touched her pain when talking… Her story.

She knew he could see beyond what she told.

He knew that.

She knew that he knew.

Numbers were exchanged.

His name was Kim.

Back in dear England.

She loved it here.

Always time for a cup of tea, and good humor.

Reflection.

She had to get a train. She had to go up north.

Up to the hills.

She had booked a small room in a hotel.

It looked cosy on the internet.

Very British.

She was catching a train 3:14 pm. She would arrive 5:22.

Perfect timing.

Katrin sat back.

Thinking about Kim.

She always felt so rich when new people suddenly arrived in her life like that.

As if they were entering with knowledge to her soul.

Her mind sometimes went into loops.

Thinking about what could be learnt from the meeting.

She had a lesson to learn about that.

That was a general issue.

To just follow the route that was laid out for her.

No patience.

They said you could learn that;

… to have patience.

She never really did.

But she learned to deal with it.

To be in a non-patience pace.

The train weaved its way through the landscape.

The sun was shining through the clouds, leaving a dark shadow on the landscape;

heavy and light at the same time.

She was reading;

at other times daydreaming.

Saw her self filled with peace.

Was it an illusion?

To ever find peace?

They said you could obtain that, if you became enlightened.

Many wanted to be so.

Did she?

Not really.

So many wannabes-enlighteners.

Could you say that? Ahhhh she didn't care.

She just wanted to feel her own inner wheel clicking into place.

The train was arriving at the train station.

She pulled out her suitcase.

Took a deep breath and made a visual scan of the location.

She went out.

It was a very small and beautiful city.
The river was on one side of the road;
houses were on the other.
She saw the hotel;
a little sweet one.
It was on the other side of the road.
It was a very old house.
She passed the street.
A dog was barking.
She hated dogs.
The sound scared her.
The whole feeling of the town… It was weird, as if she was in a completely different time zone.
She was waiting until the dogs left the front door of the hotel.
What were they saying - the dogs?
Was it a sign about the hotel?
She ignored it.

Katrin went inside the hotel; a small bell was ringing.
She felt like she was walking into a movie.
The whole illusion of time vanished.
It was as if it was real yet not real at the same time.
The hotel had a small hall; it was narrow, with coated glass on both sides of the walls.
The restaurant was on the right, the living room on the left. The reception desk was just in the front.
The ceiling was very low and there was dark wood everywhere. It was painted in dark colors and there were a lot of curtains.

"Hello, and welcome."
"Thank you."
"Did you have a nice travel?"
"Yes, thank you, very nice."

"And you are here for three nights?"

"Yes I am, I'm here for a seminar. It's such a nice town you have."

"Yes it is, thank you."

"We have a very nice little room for you, it's on the top floor. Will you be dining here this evening?"

"Yes, that would be lovely."

"The breakfast will be served here in the restaurant as well, from 6 am, and if you need anything don't hesitate to contact us in the reception, we will be here all night."

"Wonderful, thank you."

"Let Rosemary show you your room".

They passed the reception to the left and walked up the narrow stairs. Paintings were hung all over the walls, old landscapes and portraits. It was nice and cozy and very mysterious at the same time. They passed four rooms on the first floor. She glanced into one of them. There was a very dark room, with a huge wooden bed on the left. A couple was moving in. They went up one more floor. The door to her room was on the left.

"Here it is, it's not that big, but it's very cozy. You have the bathroom just over there".

"Thank you".

Katrin entered the room very slowly. Rosemary closed the door from the outside. She just stood there. There was a hatch in the ceiling, which was remarkably high in this room. The bathroom door looked like a front door and she could just barely move around in the room.

There was a weird feeling in the room.

Once again.

She ignored it.

"I will unpack my stuff and rest a bit, then go for a walk. It looked so nice by the river. God it's small in here. It's kind of sweet, but I don't like that hatch up there. The energy is disturbing. Never mind".

She went to have a shower.

Felt lust.

Masturbated.

She was laying on the bed feeling light.

Felt like she was being watched.

Did it again.

Ignored it.

Had a feeling that someone was in the room.

Felt some air moving around her.

Quickly she packed her stuff. Felt a bit of a panic.

She left the room.

Walked down the stairs.

The bell rang again.

She had left the hotel.

Outside.

She was breathing again.

Felt like she was in the "real" reality again.

Crossed the road and went down to the river.

She was listening to the water running in the river.

The dog was there again.

Barking and barking.

"It's creepy. I'm going to see if I can get a coffee somewhere".

Katrin walked along the river, feeling the rush and the strength of the river.

Her mind wandered back in time.

The river.

A tape she had heard some time ago.

An old indian woman talking about the river of life.

The wisdom of the river.

As if the river was our life.

We just had to let go and flow.

Sometimes there would be rocks as obstacles.

Sometimes it would be easy.

Sometimes hard.

Sometimes it's slow.

Sometimes it's fast.

But you just can't stand on the side of the river, you have to jump in to see where it goes, where it takes you….and deal with the ride of the water.

She had always been attracted to rivers.

Attracted to life… The uncertainty.

Yet it scared her too.

She saw a nice café.

Just by the bridge.

She went in, ordered a cappucino.

Her mind went off again. Wandered around in her daydreaming land. She felt safe here. She had done it since she was a little girl. In this world she could create anything. When she was young it was a lot of dramas, now it was projection into the future on how she would feel if she felt at home in herself.

A part of her had wanted this.

Wanted this mess she felt she had made of her soul.

It was bringing her back to her.

But it was no fun.

There was so much anxiety in this travel.

She pictured herself with her heart being able to love in a very special way. She felt the question "What is love?", knocking on her mind all the time.

She was on a journey to find out what love was.

She knew that inside.

Not that she didn't love...

But this was different.

Very.

It was a state of being she felt she could be in if she followed her way in life.

Something greater than her wanted her and she couldn't control it.

The force of the river was stronger than her own free will.

She just had to move ahead with it.

She was so angry that she had put herself in this situation.

But how could she had avoided it?

Maybe not.

Maybe she was born to be on this path, that was now a deep pain?

It made her so frustrated and at the same time she knew this was her way.

She didn't get it and at the same time she did.

The paradox of life.

Duality in a one unit world.

She glanced around the café, it was nice here. The waitress was a very sparkling woman, she was small-talking with the customers all the time, being loud and laughing behind the wooden counter full of cups and small plates with all different kinds of cake.

She felt comforted by the the abience here, not just the café with the view to the river, but by England.

She read a bit in the paper, glanced out onto the street, she could see the hotel in the back. Then felt a chill running in her bone.

She wasn't crazy about going back.

She sucked in the last bit of the energy from the café, and went back to the hotel.

A dog was there again.

A different one.

Barking out loud.

She waited again.

It left.

Ignored the inner feeling again.

Opened the door.

Went in.

The bell rang.

Timezone changed.

She was back in a Sherlock Holmes movie.

She went up to her room.

To have a bath again.

Felt the lust again.

Masturbated again.

Soon it would be supper.

She would stay at the hotel.

Eat some dinner.

And then back to sleep early.

She layed down in bed. Curled up, squeezing the quilt tight to her naked body.

Tried to relax.

Tried to avoid the constant feeling of someone being in the room with her.

She got out of bed.

Felt goosebumps on her skin.

Her hot body and the cold air in the room, clashing.
She put on her clothes.
Went downstairs.
All the doors of the rooms were closed.
She could hear voices.
Conversations.
She entered the restaurant.

It was small.
It was packed.
She got a table by the coated glass wall.

Katrin glanced around.
She felt like she was on a filmset.
As if the people at the tables were cast to sit with her at this dinner.
She was imagining how Shelock Holmes would notice all the small gestures being made at the various tables to solve the murder.

She had brought her book with her;
tried to read some pages.
The words didn't enter her mind.
She was too distracted by the whole atmosphere.
She got her fish.
It was tasty.
She ate slowly.
Watching.
Observing.
Finally she left the restaurant.
She felt the night could create a story that would carry memories.

Katrin felt an uneasy walking up the stairs.
The couple in love were on the first floor.
Did they just have a fight?
They were half in, half out of the room…
She smiled.
Walking up the last floor to her room.
The carpet was red.
She opened the door.
That hatch in the ceiling.

She brushed her teeth.
Rolled down the curtain.
Turned off the light.
Told herself that everything would be alright.

She slept.
She woke up.

"It's so scary, I'm so scared that someone is here, I can feel them. Okay, just pull the quilt up over your head. Breathe… No, no, no, no. I don't like it. They are here. Breathe, breathe. Okay if you just send out love from your heart, they can't hurt you. I heard someone saying that. I don't want to look. Breathe, breathe. Sleep, sleep".

Suddenly she couldn't take it anymore. She turned on the light again. Something so strange was going on.

She wanted to go down to the reception to talk to them and tell them she needed another room. She didn't want to stay. They said that they would be there all night.

"I just need to get down to them, then it will be alright".

She put on some clothes again, opened the door.

Felt some ease getting out of the room.

She thought for a second that she would feel safe.

She came out of the door and walked down the stairs. The windows in the hall were all open and the curtains were billowing.

She ran downstairs.

Only to find the reception empty.

No one was around.

She ran upstairs again.

And outside her door, she found her diamond earring on the floor.

She ran into the room, prayed and cried, just wanting the night to be over.

Eventually she fell asleep.

The next morning she packed her bag.

She was supposed to stay there two more nights.

She didn't care.

She didn't want to stay anymore nights there.

"Good morning."

"Good morning, did you enjoy your night?"

"No unfortunately not, something is not okay in that room, something is going on at night up there, and I don't want to stay another night, and I don't want to pay for this or the other nights."

"Okay, that's fine, I can understand. And I'm sorry to hear that."

The woman didn't argue or anything, she just said yes.

She knew about it.

That was for sure.
She had heard this before.

"Thank you, have a nice day".
"You too and safe travel".

She took her bag.
She heard the bell.
Felt she was out of the spell.

Her friends were outside in the car waiting for her.
She felt relieved.
Safe.

Later that day they learned about how some people could feel dead people, also called entities. Some had captured them on a special photoshoot.

She felt relief.

She wasn't crazy.

She could sense them, it was "real".

Still, she felt it was scary.

She didn't want to have that information in her life.

Once again, she felt that her own free will felt like it wasn't really free.

She had no free will on this journey.

Only the truth for her heart and soul, had something to say.

EIGHT

She Is Like An Italian Woman In Germany

They were four this time, four women.
They had packed their bags for the seminar.
Met in the airport.
They were excited.
She felt happy.
This time she had company.
They were going to a seminar together.
They were laughing and talking.
All very excited to go.
It was Germany this time.
They had rented a car at the airport.
Driving like Mr. Bean.
Laughing some more.
On the way, for the first time, to anyone,
she had told them about her real pain.

They had understood a little;
but not the pain.
Not really.
But could they?
She was proud of herself.
That she had dared. Dared to open up to the running river within her that she had no control over.

They arrived.
They stayed next to a field of cows.
They had laughed a lot.
There were cows, with bells around their necks.
That had made them laugh even more.
It had been dark when they arrived.
It was in the countryside.
Way out.
They had sat in a big country kitchen, wearing pajama pants, big socks and sweatshirts. Talking, drinking tea and sharing their pains.

They had a duplex apartment in a big house.
It was going to be four intense days.
You could just feel it in the air.
They had arranged buying food together.
They were like a small family.
Strange how close you can get to people in four days and then they leave for the rest of your life.
The magic of life and meetings.

"Have you been to the toilet?"
"No just go".
"Are you okay?"
"Yes I am, just looking forward to tomorrow. And you?"

"Me too, I think it's going to be really interesting. Are you nervous?"

"Yes, why?"

"You just seem so" – her friend smiled at her.

"Yes I'm actually quite nervous, I feel like I have to go through some stuff, and it feels scary. I'm also looking forward to meet the Italians again".

"Yes it seems it's very important for you".

"Yes it is... I don't know what it is about Italy, but I just feel so at home, like a part of my pain is being able to heal in Italy. It sounds strange that's it a country, but it's like that, I just have to see what is going to happen".

"And your friend?" Her friend winked at her, smiling.

"He's just special, he has a key to something. I feel I have met him before, that he is important".

"Hmmm, I know what you mean".

"And I just have to follow it…"

She thought about her Italian friend whom she had met once before Venice. They had kept in contact over the past months. She thought about him, and was looking forward to meeting him. There was something about him, not in a romantic kind of way, but like his soul had something, something she had to explore, as if this relationship had a key to unlock part of her pain.

She often saw relationships and events in life as patterns, like the game Tetris. When the energies matched they could release the dust on the shelves of the souls.

It was important to be open to those well-matched relationships. Not that it would necessarily be easy because of the match. It just meant that something in the soul was calling. She could never avoid that voice. It was so noisy.

And if she tried; her body would demand pay back immediately.

As a friend had once said to her: "You always end up doing it anyway, so why don't you just do it?"

She was glad that one of her friends was with her on this trip. She had a comforting feeling.

They went to bed.

It felt like when you were a child and on a school trip; no one really wanting to sleep.

Just giggling.

Small talking.

Eventually the dream world arrived.

Morning came.

They woke up.

Laughing again at the thought of yesterday.

They were all excited.

They said "Good morning" to the cows.

They got into the car.

Drove to the seminar.

It was a huge seminar, lots of people.

She felt her stomach tighten up a bit.

Took a deep breath.

She knew something had to change in this seminar.

It only took her a moment to realize that it was not just a feeling.

"Hi, who are you? I'm the teacher".

"Hi, I'm Katrin".

He was looking at her body, scanning her.

She could feel it.

"You're going to get a lot out of the seminar? You have got a Kundalini going on".

Katrin looked at him and she knew that he had seen it, seen her pain and he had said the exact word. He was the only one to ever recognize and speak of it.

He smiled and left or maybe he began speaking to her friend.

She couldn't remember.

She felt a bit amazed, glad, excited, scared.

The last minute before start;
the Italians arrived.
Her friends were here.
They came over and hugged and smiled.
She felt like a huge gift was here for her.
The presence of their energy brought out a strength in her.
Like the hidden energy of Italy would carry her through.

Her friend saw her at the same moment she saw him.
He came over and they hugged;
happy to see each other.

"Ciao."
"Ciao, Luca".
"How are you? So good to see you again".
"So good, had too much wine yesterday".
"Yeah, you do look a bit hung-over, I must say. Did you have a nice trip?"
"Yes it was great".

They paused and smiled.

"I think we're starting now, let's talk later".
"Yes, let's talk then, I'm sitting with others, ciao".

The seminar began.
It was not a boring one, they were learning a lot.
Slowly.
Hour by hour.
She felt an uneasiness getting closer to her body.
The body reacted.
Showing her pain.
She was scared.
The teacher promised to be there for her.
She was scared anyway.
At one point;
they made an agreement.
If she allowed herself to let go;
he would come, whenever she needed him.

He kept his promise.
Slowly her guard came down.

It was lunch.
They met there.
Her friends.
The Italians.
There was a line.
To get food.
They were talking;
about Italy.
Waiting for their turn.
Laughing.
They came back to the table.
Luca said to one of the Italians.

"Do you know what? She's like an Italian woman".
"I know that, but how?"

They were all laughing.
Katrin felt at home.
Something in her felt like she reach a part of what people would call home.
She had never felt at home anywhere.
But Italy?!
What was it?
Why?
She knew that there was a lesson to be learned.
Because when something is so strong, you have to learn.
You have to own it yourself.
Otherwise others have to carry that sense.
She was not looking for that.
She was looking for her pain to vanish.
She enjoyed feeling free and happy for a moment.
Eating with her friends and Italy.
She was like an Italian woman.
That part of her.
She had to get to know that part.
For sure.
How could she not?

They went back to the seminar.
Time to let go.

They did an exercise.
She fully let go.
They were more than a handful.
Holding her in the air.
She showed her pain.

Fully.
She felt supported by something bigger.
Now it was out.
For the first time;
the pain materialized.

The teacher said that it was good that she had done it.
What she had done.
Was showing her life energy.
Could that be so bad?
In a way it was so beautiful.
That was the catch.
She was so scared.
So scared of her own life energy.
The one that she ought to love.
Nurture.
And what she had done was to hide.
Suppress
With all her might.
And now it was open and out.

She was exhausted by the end of the day.
She was sitting on a table.
Staring out in the air.
One of the Italians said.

"Are you ok?"
"I don't know".

One came silent over to her and held her.
Their energy was healing.
Even when she had shown her worst;
they were there.

Finally something could start moving in a different direction in life.

Her friends were there and they went back to their house together.

They were so fantastic.

She had a steak.

Went to bed.

Tucked in.

She had done well.

Being an Italian woman.

Letting go of her pain.

She felt heavy and light.

When her head

Touched her pillow.

She slept.

She was dreaming about a snake.

A snake that was not locked up anymore.

She had dared to see the eyes of the snake.

It was time for them to start melting together.

In the end there was only one thing to own.

Her snake.

The next days were exhausting and liberating at the same time.

She processed a lot.

Hung out with the Italians.

They were good days.

She was tired after the seminar.

Happy and relieved.

She had made a huge turn.

In facing her pain.

It was a pain.

But it was hers.

And her energy.

She was proud.

She smiled to herself.

When the airplane went into the dark skies and left Germany.

Katrin arrived home.

Sat down.

Reflected.

Felt more grounded than in a long time.

Her feeling of being more whole was strong.

She wrote a small message to the teacher on Messenger.

She was happy and grateful for him.

He had dared

More than anyone.

To take her to the next step in her healing process.

She knew that she had to call that guy Kim now.

They guy she had met on the plane to England.

He had offered her something.

An energy space that she could feel was right.

She had not been ready at that time.

Now it was the time to open up for that road.

This trip had helped her.

Opened her up.

So she could face the pain.

She was also aware that Italy was so important.

But how? What? When? And where?

She had always dreamt about having sex and arguing in Italian.

You have to be careful what you wish for.

She didn't know that eventually that dream would come true.

One month later another seminar was scheduled to be in Italy.

Once again she knew that she had to go.

Italy, Italy... the words were looping in her head.

NINE

Someone Transforms Into An Angel

It was Celia's birthday, they had invited 100 people and they were going to have a big party in the garden. Celia would do a bit of the cooking, but the whole family would be there to support her. It was a big task, but they were doing it together. She loved it.

They had set up a tent in the garden. Fabio was home to help prepare it all. She hadn't seen him all that much lately. He was always travelling with his job.

She had felt quite alone for a while. The older boys studied in other cities so it was just herself and Angelo most of the time. Not that she didn't enjoy it, but still.

She felt lucky that Giovanni was around a lot; it warmed her heart.

He knew her better than Fabio did. He somehow always knew how she felt, just one look and he knew…

"Celia, Celia where are you my darling?"… Her sister was calling her, with a big smile on her face.

"I'm here my darling… I just drifted a bit." She smiled back and hugged her sister.

"I'm so glad you're here. I've missed you".

"I've missed you too my darling Celia. How are you? Is everything okay? You look happy but also tired!"

"I'm okay. I'm glad and sometimes tired. So yes you're right. Do you know if they have put the meat on the grill outside?"

"Si, si – everything is okay my darling"

Her sister danced away with two big plates of salad.

Celia hadn't felt like sharing her thoughts.

Tonight she just wanted to have fun and forget the dark inner cloud.

She heard it now.

The front door kept opening.

She smiled.

She went out to all the guests.

Everyone were hugging and kissing.

"Ciao", "Ciao".

"Bella", "Bella".

So much noise.

So nice.

Today would be a fantastic celebration.

She felt the joy.

She was fifty.

Giovanni caught her eyes.

He smiled warmly.

He knew she was so happy right now.

She kept eye contact with him for a long while.

She smiled back.

He was special.

"I'm so happy he's in my life".

Angelo was excited. He had been at work all day.

Giovanni had made him a special sort of manager in the shop.

He took his responsibilities very serious.

He was working every day.

Sometimes in the shop; sometimes in the wine bar.

But every day.

He was very proud and everyone who came to the shop, loved him.

He lit up the shop with his sunshine.

Everyone called him Sunshine boy

No one cared if he had Downs.

He was Angelo, the Angel boy, the Sunshine boy.

They treated him like he was an addition to their life.

Not at deficit.

In the shop he;

Smiled a lot.

Talked a lot.

Swore a lot.

Spoke out loud every thought on his mind.

Did his job.

Paid attention to everyone.

Loved everyone.

Hugged a lot.

Had a temper.

Giovanni's pride.

He was now 23.

He was excited that Mama had a party.

He loved when there was so much love and sharing.

He found Luca and Giuseppe in the garden.

They laughed and hugged;
so happy to see each other.

Celia watched her boys.
Her heart was swelling up.
Her boys.
She caught Luca eyes.
He smiled warmly.
He knew.
She knew.
The love.
A guest came over to greet her.
Her eyes left the boys.
It was the last time she saw them together in their human form.

The phone was ringing.
Anna picked it up.

Luca had been worried all day for what seemed to be no reason. He had been short in his sentences, absent. He felt worried, he said he was worried but he couldn't say why.

"Si, it's Anna".
"Yes, hang on".

She looked at Luca. Her eyes were serious; she never took them away from his eyes.
His eyes were big now.
He got scared.
He knew that this was not a good call.

"It's for you, my dear".

She stretched her arm across the table, handing him the phone. He starred at the phone, then at her.

"Take it, it's for you" she tried to smile.

But they both knew.
It was not good news.

Luca starred at the phone.

"Pronto!"
"Si".
"No I don't want to sit down".

Anna looked at him in despair. She could hear the desperation in his voice. His eyes opened wider and his posture tightened up.

"NO!"
"NO!"
"NO!"
"NO!"
"NO!"
"NO!"

Luca was walking around the room.
The NO grew.
Louder and louder.
One could
Hear
The fight

Against
The devastating news.
Refusing
The truth.
Refusing
The facts.
That his beloved
Brother.
Had just died.
23 years old.

His mother was on the other end.
Shock, despair.
She said
Giovanni was there.
Luca hung up.
The feeling was too much.
Too unreal.
Like he had died himself.

Anna looked at him.

"What happened?"

But she knew.
Angelo had died.

"What happened? What happened, tell me darling".

Luca walked around screaming Noooooooooooo, crying out loud. He was here, but not here. She tried to get close to him, but he wouldn't, he couldn't let her in. He felt like he couldn't breathe.

"What happened? Please Luca tell me, tell me!"

Anna moved closer to him, wanted to hold him, but he wouldn't let her.

Then, just out of the tears, he mumbled:

"He is dead,
He is dead,
He had a heart attack,
In the wine bar…
There was nothing they could do…
He died instantly.
Giovanni was there.
He held him".

He was looking at her now.

"What am I to do?
How can I live without him?
Mama was so devastated.
I couldn't talk to her.
I can't talk to her now.
How can I get through this?"

He was now crying.

Water was running.
Running down her cheeks too.
Slowly she got closer to him.
She held him.
Held him close into her.
He relaxed for a moment.

Let her hold him.
Wished that she could remove his pain.
He had been right all day.
Right, that something was wrong.
Like he knew that something bad was going to happen.
She didn't say anything.
They cried together.

Then he left.
Took his phone.
It was ringing.
The family.
All of his friends.
Everyone knew now.
The phone took the messages.
He couldn't let the world in.
The phone became his wall.
His wall against the world.
The phone could absorb the pain.
Only for now.
He wished he could disappear.
Keep the world as it was some minutes ago.
Keep the silence.
Not to talk to anyone.
Not hearing that the unbearable had happened.
Again and again.
Not wanting to hear the truth.
His dear Angelo.
How could it be real?
He took the car.
Drove to the sea.
Screaming.

Screaming to GOD.
"How could you?"

There was no reply.
Only silence.
Like God didn't even have an answer.

Luca laid down in his bed.
He cried and cried.
The deep, deep pain.
That he had no idea how to ever be able to live with.
He was unstoppable.
The tears would not stop.
Anna was there.
She didn't know what to do.
Was quiet beside him.
Tried to hold him.
He still wouldn't let her.
He couldn't.
He was exhausted.
Angelo, no longer here.
No more laughing.
No more tears.
Only his own now.
He felt sleep taking over his consciousness.
He was letting go of the day.

In the night.
He woke up.
He felt it.
He felt him.

He saw him.
He was just around him.
Touching his face with his hands.
He heard him, it was clear.

"I'm okay brother".
"I'm okay".
"I will always be here".
"Be strong".
"I love you".

Luca was completely silent, and then he burst into tears when he disappeared.
Angelo had been here.
Held him.
Angelo was now an angel.

TEN

Love, Love, Love

Katrin dialed his number. Her hands were shaking; heart was beating…

Ring,
Ring,
Ring,
She was just about to hang up, already had an excuse ready in her head.

"It was not meant to be, it's probably better not to, I'm not sure whether this would be good or not".

"Hi, it's Kim".

He had a slow, fine voice. It was so soft.

She remembered him right away; saw his face in her inner picture bank. He had such a slow fine pace, so calm and such a beautiful smile.

"Hi, it's me… from the plane…"

She felt the air was dense and a thousand minutes were passing in one.
She didn't want to explain too much.

"I remember your voice… from England right?"

She could hear his smile through the phone.

"Yes, it's me".

She paused.
Didn't know how to put it.

"You said… I mean… my pain… you could help me?"

She blushed behind the phone.

"How could you ask such a question, arghhh what is he going to say? I mean this is so weird, he did message me saying: you have inner pain. But it's so embarrassing" She was literately hitting herself for being stupid".

But he didn't respond to her inner thoughts.
He was glad she called.

"Yes, let's book a day, and see where it takes us".
"Yes, thanks", she felt humbled.

They agreed,
about the date.
She put it in her calendar.
They hung up.
She felt scared.
She felt light.
It was a place for healing.
She knew
Deep within.
Then the doubt
Worries
Entered her mind.
But who's to say that it would be better?
She tried to be positive.
Be positive about who she was.
If only she could get rid of the pain.
It would be the best.
She had a day now.
It would be good.
It would be sad.
He would be there.
Be there for her pain.
He would talk.
And show her.
With his hands.
With his heart.
Her body.
Her senses.
The energy
They called love.
But at this point
She
Didn't

Know
Any of this.

He had said so many beautiful things about life on the plane.
Carefully watching her all the time.
Taking his time to answer.
Taking his time to listen.
He smiled a lot.
He had laughed whole-heartedly, when he answered about his job.
"I listen a lot," he had said.
She had asked why.
Many hearts come to me; often they are in pain.
She had asked if he was a therapist.
He had smiled.
No I work with hearts.
With my hands.
Love.
Massage;
it's Tantra.

He had smiled.
She had smiled.
At that point.
In the silence between them.
She had felt.
That he could see her.
See beyond her.
Look right into that place.
She called it her pain.
Others would call it something different.

The guru's in India would have definitely referred to it differently.

She didn't care.

She had her pain.

He had said the word love.

She felt that he could see the intense constant feeling of sexual energy in her.

But it was as if he hadn't cared about that.

She knew he had seen her soul.

She hadn't said anything.

She had looked away.

Felt very private.

She had felt it.

He was important.

She knew that.

Time would reveal the journey they would take together.

Yet again… her impatience;

eager to see instant results.

But what is a result?

And when is it good?

Depends entirely on the eyes of the beholder.

The day came when the name "Kim" was in the calendar. It was autumn, windy and raining, she had just gotten home from Germany when she had called him; she had known in Germany that it was time to go. The unknown higher source was calling her on a quest for understanding love, and she knew when to listen very carefully. She never had a choice; her body just told her immediately if she wasn't true to herself. She was one of those people who listened when it talked. It actually had many really good points, that body of hers. Just as much as she was looking forward to it, she was afraid to go, but she knew that she had to enter the door into her own inner fear and find out where it would lead.

Katrin parked her car, turned the key. The motor stopped. The noise of the engine stretching itself after the trip was heard vaguely in the background.

She took a deep breath, glancing towards the building.

Looked down.

Took her bag.

Took her phone.

Looked at it.

Checked Facebook.

Looked out again.

Felt restless.

She had plenty of time,

Too much time.

She reached for the phone again, looked at the clock.

It was time.

She took one last deep breath.

Opened the door.

Glanced to see if any cars where coming before she crossed the road.

None.

She walked, tried to feel contained.

Tried to breath.

She walked slowly.

Opened the outer door.

Walked up the stairs… slowly.

Smelled the odor of the stairs.

Walked to the door.

Rang the bell.

The minutes felt like hours.
The door opened.
He was
Just there in front of her.
She hesitated a bit.
Took the step into the new world.
She looked and looked away at the same time.

"Hi".

He smiled and his soft tone made her feel welcomed.

"Hi".

It was strange, she was nervous.
It was warm.
It was dark.
It was soft.
She felt comforted by the walls.
She wanted to run.
She wanted to stay.
She wanted to be helped.
He was happy to see her.
Followed her to the room.
He listened to her words.
The pain
That had been there for so many years.
There was enough space in the room.
Enough space to be yourself: in whatever form that was.

They began a journey:
a long one.
He showed her.

The way into herself.
With his body.
With his hands.
His heart.
He peeled off the layers of anxiety and dust.
Over time.
With his patience.
He showed her how to use her energy to open up.
Open up to life.
Open up to love.
The tears were many.
The awareness of the senses increasing.
Making life more present.
GOD came closer.
Feeling;
accepting the whole of her.
Her love.
Her heart.
Her soul.
He held her, in every part that was needed for growth.

"Use your energy, use it in every part of your life. Use that wonderful life energy you have, be present with your friends and family, and be present with you work, open up for it. The energy, the one you call your pain. It's you. It wants you".

She was lying all exhausted in his arms, he held her really tight. She felt her heart, she felt his heart, she felt love. She felt so exhausted and so happy, the feeling of this love, was beautiful. Tears ran down her cheeks. Her body had let go completely, the memory of what it had done was already gone, but the feeling of the energy in her back was crawling up towards her head, the inner picture of the snake merging with her body, her very own snake. She had remembered the snake from many years ago. She had picked it up in the woods, in a visualization at a seminar many years ago, the snake was her. She hadn't realized then, but now it all fell into place. The snake was her! And she had spent so many years trying to lock it up, to throw it away when it was just really showing her true self.

She looked at him. How was he able to see that the thing she called her pain, was actually the most beautiful part of her? It was her. Her life energy.

She had pushed it away, hated it, wanted it to go away and now he was teaching her to love it. Love that strong vibrant energy that was overwhelming her body, in lust, anger, fear, happiness and a huge strong need to answer her quest for love.

"You have such a beautiful heart, use it. Let it out. Don't hide. Love, Love, Love always Love. Love is everything, don't be scared".

Katrin was crying really heavily know, not from sorrow, but for this immense feeling of love that was expanding her heart. She was opening up to it. The physical heart was stretching to find a new form.

Love.
Love.

Love.

She left that day.
With a new saying in her heart.
When ever she felt in pain.

She said the words to herself.

Love.
Love.
Love.

What she didn't know was that those three words were going to be so important, in her continued quest for love.

She had only just begun.

ELEVEN

Back In Italy

It was the first time she had been to Italy in January.

It was freezing cold.

The wind cut through to her bones so much it hurt.

It was not Italy at it's best.

Always known for the sun and warmth.

She had returned.

The invitation had come through her mailbox.

Unexpected.

Like small seeds that were laid out on her road.

Just to follow.

She only had to pick them up.

Go with them.

In an email the teacher had said she needed this seminar in order to accomplish something.

So she had come.

It had turned out that she really didn't need the seminar anyway.

The teacher had smiled and said it was a mistake.

The information was wrong.

Something had just wanted her to go.

She needed to come.

Funny how small circumstances make such a huge impact in the bigger scale of things.

And yet we tend to think that only the big events count.

Life is funny that way.

She reflected.

One teacher could write just one sentence. And upon that you make a decision.

That can then change your life.

When small actions feel greater than the big, it can make the whole wheel of life, turn in another direction.

It's amazing.

Katrin took a taxi into the center of Venice.

It was her second time that year.

The taxi stopped just at the border, where cars are not permitted.

She paid the driver.

Gave him a tip.

She was going to be here for six days.

She walked through the city with her suitcase. Amazed by it. As all other people were. Have you ever heard anyone say that Venice is crap?

She saw a boat coming to get all the garbage in the city. She smiled to herself.

The shops, the small bridges, the small hidden corners and the restaurants were everywhere. She smiled to herself again, realizing that she was walking here in Venice.

Life was truly amazing.

When she just listened to her inner voice, it was as if some majestic force was guiding her from within.

It was only when, doubts, anxiety and worries entered her mind that she closed down from that magical inner melody of life.

She was walking down toward Piazza San Marco, to take a boat from there to get to the small Island where the seminar was going to be held this time. She was freezing now.

First she needed to go and see when the boat was leaving.

30 minutes to go.

She went to a café.

"Ciao".

"Ciao, could I have a chocolate?"

"Si".

"Ehhh, caldo e freddo?"

"ejjjjj. Caldo – I think!"

She was smiling to him now. She had learned it, but always doubted herself.

He was laughing now, and made a gesture with his hands and face, showing her that it means warm.

"Si, si" – she was laughing too.

He spoke with some of the other guests in the bar; they were laughing now and smiling at her.

"I just love to hear them talk, and express the language with their body. I feel so at home here. I wish I could speak it. It feels like the whole language is in my body. As if I was born with the chip code to this language. I just need to take the time to sit down and do it. So much I want to do all the time".

"Sette Euro".
"Ok, Grazie".

Katrin sat down at a table and watched the boats. Seven Euros, I think this cup of chocolate is paid then. She smiled to herself. She felt the warm of the café was sinking into her bones now. She relaxed a bit more. Breathing slowly, drinking the warm chocolate in small sips, landing in Venice.

It was time to go to the boat. She left the café.

"Ciao".
"Ciao, Ciao, arrivederci".
"Arrivederci".

The cold wind was back.
She walked along the wharf down to the last boat.
It was arriving now.
She hopped onboard.

He pulled in the robes.
The boat left.
It was a short ride.
She looked back.
Watching the houses of Venice getting smaller.

Soon they arrived at the island.

They got off.

There were many huge buildings on the island.

In the old days it had been a monastery.

Later it had been used for mentally ill people.

Now it was a place for seminars etc.

She was shown to her room.

They passed a beautiful garden.

She could easily get a mental image of all the monks, taking care of the garden.

They went to one of the buildings furthest away at the back of the island.

The buildings were massive.

They entered the building.

The halls were wide and the ceilings high.

It echoed a lot.

She felt an unease crawling into her bones.

She could hear the screams in the walls.

They carried many unpleasant stories.

They had seen a lot:

those walls.

She saw a long row of wooden doors like the small chambers of a prison.

He showed her the room.

It was dark.

Very modest.

Almost too modest.

It was cold.

He said she should turn on the heater.

It was so cold.

Freezing cold.

He left.
She felt so scared when he closed the door.
Like in a prison.
She tried to relax.
But it was so freezing cold
She just didn't want to be there.
In her mind
She already knew.
She was not going to stay in this room.
It was creepy.
After 30 minutes.
She left the room.
Went to the reception.

"Ciao".
"Ciao, I just got a room and there is no heat in it. I want another room. It's so cold".
"Of course mam, I will look into it".

"I just want out of that room. I don't want to stay there, that's for sure. They are not making me stay there. Just the thought of the room makes me feel uneasy; it felt like it was dead that room; like someone really sick had stayed there and still is. Please let it be easy to get another room".

"We can help you, just follow me in 10 minutes and I will give you another room".
"Grazie".

"Hi".

She looked back; some friends from an earlier seminar had arrived.

"Hi, how good to see you. Did you have a nice trip?"

"Yes, sure. Good to see you too. What's happening?"

"Oh, I just got a very cold room, and I need a new one."

"Yes, it's really cold here. I think we're going out for dinner tonight. Do you want to join us?"

"Yes, that would be lovely. Do you know what time?"

"No, but I will let you know".

"Thank you, see you later. Ciao".

"Ciao, ciao".

She followed him to the building near the back again.
She had hoped for another building.
They were just walking up one floor.
It was the same kind of room.
Very modest; but with a warm feeling.
She felt,
Not safe,
But safer.

"Ciao, ciao".

He left.
She had a bath.
A long one.
Laid down on the bed.
Put on some relaxing music.
Felt the warmness entering her bones.
She started to relax and fell asleep.

She woke an hour later.
Time for dinner.
They took the boat to Venice center.
They were eight.

They were having a lot of fun.
She practiced some Italian words.
"Pepe".
"Sale".
She was repeating them after an Italian woman.
They applauded her.
She loved the excitement.

One guy in the group looked intensely at her.
He knew her from the other seminars.

"You have a thing with the Italians".
"I know. Do you know what?"
"No, we just have to see, why you're here, but you have something here".

She felt happy and relieved that she was not the only one feeling it.
It felt nice that he could see it too.
That there was more to it than just some trips to Italy.
Something of great importance.

The Seminar started the next day.
She walked through the big corridor.
In her mind she saw the monks walking though them.
Felt their presence and the pain of the place at the same time.

Luca was here.
They hadn't spoken in a long time.
It was good to see him again.
She still had a feeling that there was something to learn from this friendship.
There it was again.

Her feeling of impatience.

Patience just wasn't her style.

Why couldn't she just get the information quickly and then leave?

She basically didn't like it when she had to stay and come back to places where it didn't make sense. She felt stupid for always having to listen to her heart. She debated a lot with herself on this one. Why was it not a practical heart she had? Why did she have to live a life where she had to do crazy things like travelling to Italy to learn something about her pain? Why couldn't she just have a simple life? She always wanted that, but in her core she knew she would never get it. And yet she was happy in a way with that too, because that was who she was.

Life was crazy.

She smiled to herself.

Too many thoughts, going around and around and around and…

Katrin had her writings with her.

She tried to capture the pain in some drawings that described it.

Maybe it would be easier for people to understand.

The pattern of the human being she saw.

Maybe not.

Maybe it was just easier for her.

Who really knew?

She was sitting at the breakfast table.

There were a lot of people.

But no one from the seminar this morning.

Strange.

She sat down.

Luca was suddenly here.

It was so weird with him.

He often popped.
From out of nowhere.
It was just the two of them.
He glanced at her writing.
He didn't comment on it.
They started eating.
They were talking about their families.
Where they were raised and much more.
He came from Pitigliano.
She didn't know where it was
Tuscany.
She asked if he had any siblings.
He had had two.
Angelo was his name, the other Giuseppe.
His sorrow touched his throat while speaking.
About Angelo.
He had died.
From a heart attack.
He was only 23.
He spoke about him.
That he had been a very special person,
with a lot of special friends.
It was a huge sorrow.
He didn't even have to tell her.
She could feel that.

They walked towards the seminar room.
When Luca was taking about his brother.
She felt a strong connection towards his brother.
She had no idea why.
She felt happy that he had shared the story.
Had shared something very private.
Why did she feel that strong connection to those two?

What was there to learn?
Time would tell.

The seminar had already started.
It had been a magical morning.
The sound of the journey.
The sound of life.
Made sense without making sense.
She just had to go with it.

TWELVE

Arriving In Rome

"We will be landing soon. We all hope you had a pleasant flight and for those who are here to visit, we wish you a nice stay and for those who are returning home, welcome home".

The moment the stewardess said home, the wheels scratch the surface of Roman ground and she whispered to herself. *"I'm home"*, and her body relaxed more than it had ever done. From a place within so deep and unknown, like a part of her self was at home here. At home in Rome.

"What was that? From where did that feeling come? I have never felt at home anywhere in the world and then this, Rome. I hate Rome. Remember when you were on Interrail? And at the same time I feel a deep joy within. Could it really be that I could feel at home, learn how to feel at home here in life?"

The mixture of excitement, joy and the uncertainty of what it all meant, rushed through her body.

She stayed in her seat.

She was sitting at the back.

Looked out through the windows.

Watched all the passengers standing.

Eager to get out.

She knew that feeling too.

She had risen quickly from the seat sometimes herself.

Right now.

She just sat.

Watching the plane starting to be emptied.

It was her turn.

She went out.

"Ciao".

"Ciao, Ciao".

The Stewardess's smiled.

She felt the heat, the special warm light of Rome, and the dry smell of Rome hitting her senses.

She absorbed it.

Went to the toilet.

Had a cappuccino in the cafe by the luggage belt.

Luggage was late.

In Rome no one was really busy.

They eventually got their suitcases.

Went out.

Her name was on a piece of paper.

A driver was there.

There was water and peanuts in the backseat.

The Mercedes left the terminal.

She was heading towards the hotel.

Katrin looked out the windows, watching the dust, stone pine trees, cars, people, the shimmering heat, she was just absorbing everything with her whole being, every cell was open to all the impressions.

The driver knew his way. Luckily he was silent. She was happy to avoid the small talk. She was not in the mood for that.

She arrived at the hotel. It was a nice one. So was the room. She had one day to see Rome.

"Ciao, can you help me?"
"Ciao, of course Madam. What can I do for you?"
"I would love to see Rome today. But I have only got the rest of the day! – is it possible?"

She smiled.
The receptionist smiled – bent down and took a map.
Looked at his watch.

"Yes Madam it is" – he smiled warmly.
"Do you like to walk?"
"Yes I do?
"Okay so this is what you do!"

He took his pen and he circled it all. The Coliseum, Piazza Venezia, Fontana di Trevi, Piazza di Spagna, Piazza Navona, The Pantheon, etc.

"You have go to the "tabaccheria" and buy a train ticket, it cost 1,50 Euro and then take the metro. Get off at Coliseum. Then you can begin your trip. All the famous buildings in Rome are quite near each other, so you will be able to see a lot."

"Grazie, that is so great".
"Prego".

She was looking at the map tuning into the route. Looked at him, smiled.

"Arrivederci".
"Arrivederci".

She did as he had told her and she arrived at the Coliseum. As she exited the Metro, she was completely overwhelmed by the sight of the building.

"Rome, why? Why are you so strong in me? I thought I hated you. I wish that I lived here. I wish that I were born here; I wish you could tell me the longing I feel can be healed here. What can you do for me? Why are you so strong?"

She stepped out watched the Coliseum, absorbed it, watched the people and soaked up the sun. The costumed Italians looking like fake warriors from years gone by. She slowly walked towards the centre; once in a while looking back to see the Coliseum, as if it was the only time she would see it.

She walked fast; she had a lot to see in a short time. She smiled as she tuned into Rome, who was Rome? She found a small street, Via del Governo Vecchio, near Piazza Navona, there were several small restaurants and wine bars. She picked out hers; it would become *her* wine bar. She ordered a glass of Pinot Noir, water and Melazane. The wine bar played awful music, but the ambience was wonderful. It was packed. They sat close to each other around small wooden tables draped in white and red squared tablecloths. Candles and snacks were on the tables too.

Katrin took her book, had a sip of the wine, observed the Italians. When she observed them she felt so far away from them, but inside her, in her soul, she felt that a part of her belonged here. She felt such a strong connection. She was amazed that it was possible to feel so connected to a country, to a lot of people whom you have no relationship to. It amazed her, puzzled her, made her happy and made her curious. Her soul relaxed in a way it had never done before.

"I have to come here, I have to be here much more. I need to feel these feelings many times. I wish that I could live here, but I know I can't, but I could travel. Just wait and see. But I need come".

She was arguing with herself. Trying to make sense of the feeling, trying to stop the voice in her that just wanted to be here. But she knew she would not have a choice in the perspective of the soul. When it had spoken she would have to listen. She knew.

She was reading.
Half daydreaming.
Took a sip of her wine.
Ate small bites.
Watched some more.
Felt the tiredness.
That only comes when you let go from deep within.
She asked to pay.
He asked why she was here.
She answered him.

The truth she kept as a secret.
The darkness of the Roman night.
Had captured the skies.
The ambiences changed.
People were enjoying the pasta.
The wine.
The street sales guys selling plastic neon lights
People laughing.
Talking.
Celebrating life.
Some had a lot to say.
Some sat in silence.
As if they had lost the ability to share.
She walked slowly.
Time to go to the hotel.
She walked the stairs to her room.
Took of her clothes.
Watched her naked self in the mirror.
Brushed her teeth.
Felt the blanket on her skin.
Sleep surrounded her.
Taking her away from the day.
Leaving her in the bed.
With the night to process the day.
Tomorrow she would be with the Italians.

Morning came, she was stretching, sat on the side of the bed, touched her legs slowly up and down. Watched her toes moving. Her feet landed on the carpet, she stood up. Slowly she pulled the curtains to the side. She had a nice view from fifth floor over the pool, Rome was there in front of her, wakening with good coffee to be enjoyed and croissants to be eaten. The buzz of a new Roman day had begun.

She ordered room service for breakfast.
She was reading and eating, waiting for the time to pass, so she could join the seminar. She was ready.

Luca was there.
They hugged.
"So good to see you again how are you?"
"I'm really good, thank you. So good to see you too. Do you like it here?"

He smiled in his own cheeky way, when he knew that she was just in the right spot.

"Yes you know, it's amazing here. Something is so special here in Rome, as I feel I'm home".

He looked at her smiled.

"You're an Italian girl, you know".

She smiled. They had a connection, as if she had known him before in another life, with an unspoken language that she knew he was also aware of.

She sat down.
Had a glass of water.
Enjoyed the Italian words flying around the room.
The seminar had started.
She had a session.
She had asked.

"What is it with me and Italy?"

The answered had been that time will tell.
She closed her eyes.
Feeling the sorrow.
The deep pain again.
Many tears flowing from her eyes.
One day nearly not making it.
It hadn't stopped.
The crying.
The pain.
The longing to belong.
Somewhere within her.
She knew.
She was not even near.
But she was closer.
She had fallen in love.
In love with a town.
A new chapter had begun.
The title was.
ROME.

THIRTEEN

An Angel Arrives

The friendship had started to blossom. Luca and her started to write more frequently sharing their passion for growth, the quest of life, and the quest of love. They had a strong connection, they both recognized, and her love for her friend increased. It was a special love. She didn't want him as a lover, but her soul had a strong love for him, as she had to live and share something with him in this lifetime, again.

She didn't know what she was doing, and she felt so stupid having this love for him. She wanted it to be taken it away, but she knew she had to go through it. There was a lesson to be learned from their friendship.

"But how can you say you love someone, when you don't want this person? And do you need to tell them your love in order for the love to be real? How can you show them your love?"

She felt a strong force within and she didn't like that. It was the same deep intensity she felt with Rome. It scared her, too much of it exhausted her. It drained her; no good could come out of it.

The quest of love always ran the show called life. That exhausting life play she had been forced to continually perform…

When the pain of the quest was too much, she always heard Kim's soft voice in her inner ear. "Love, Love, Love". It was as if it gave fuel to her quest, as she was better able to handle it then.

They had long philosophical talks about life and the lessons they learned along the way. The many challenges to be faced and how to deal with them.

Luca called one day, he was so excited he had just learnt a new technique for cleansing the soul's pain.

"Ciao."
"Ciao, Come stai?"
"Bene, e tu?"
"Bene, Bene".

They laughed, she was trying to speak some Italian words once in a while, she felt she had the language in her body, hidden like an old treasure, but releasing the knowledge wasn't at all easy.

"I have learned a new technique this weekend. I have been away on a seminar to learn how to use essential oils to cleanse the soul. It's so powerful, you should try, and it's so beautiful.

I have had the most amazing insights all weekend. Do you want to try?"

"Si, it would be amazing".

Katrin had been in Rome for a couple of days. She had found a hotel where she stayed every time that she was there. It had become a part of her life, to travel to Rome to heal. She had made the decision and it was good, she was confused about it, but it was good. Luca and her were sitting in a bar eating a pizza slice. Luca and the owner were good friends. She had picked a couple of different slices. Potatoes, squash, garlic and mozzarella with tomatoes.

The restaurant was really ugly, but the pizzas were fantastic.

"So tell me more about it. How does it work and do I have to do anything?"

"Well, you need to give me some personal stuff and then I create the right formula for you".

"What do you mean by stuff?"

"I need some of your hair and your signature".

"Ah, I see".

"Yes, then I can work out what you need for the bath, what oils and salts would be good, maybe even crystals. But we will see".

"What does it do? It cleanses you right? I like that, getting rid of the mud".

"Yes it is really great".

I would love to do that. Will you send it to me, when I'm back home?"

"Sure, that sounds like a great idea".

"Let's go, I'm ready".

They ate the rest of their meal, paid and left the restaurant.

They drove the longest route.
20 kilometers down to the sea.
They stopped.
Ate an ice cream.
The best ice cream.
She had coconut and strawberry.
He had chocolate and banana.
They walked along the beach.
The sun was about to call it a day.
It was so big.
So red.
Many people had come for the same view of the sunset.
They sat down in the sand.
Ate their ice cream.
In silence.
Watched the big red one.
Slowly.
Sinking into the sea.
When they were done.
They did a meditation.
Breathing in.
The air.
The heartbeat.
The sun's goodbye.
The present moment.

God! Italians and getting things done. She couldn't stop smiling, but it had taken a month since she got back home from her last visit and the oil had not yet arrived. Jasmine was the name of the oil.

"Jasmine, Jasmine, Jasmine, dear Jasmine" She was talking out loud to herself. The oil had almost become a person and Luca was getting more and more frustrated that the oil was not available out of Italy. "Italians" he yelled down the phone when they spoke.

In the end she had planned to go to Rome again and she would get the oil once she got there.

She landed in Rome and was quite excited, it felt like the formula and special bath treatment that Luca had devised was going to be important in some way.

"Jasmine, who are you? Why do you make me so happy, when I haven't even met you? And why is it so difficult to meet. I can't wait, and why am I talking to an oil?"

She was smiling to herself, had just landed and gotten her car. She was to go and buy a crystal for the bath. She made a quick stop at Luca's and picked up the oil. Both relieved that she finally had received Jasmine.

"Have fun and I'll see you tomorrow" were his last word before she closed the door.

It was evening now, nice dinner at her special wine bar. She always ordered the same Melanzane alla parmigiana and a glass of Pinot Noir. She had felt relaxed, and was looking forward to the bath.

Katrin came back to the hotel, put on some nice healing music and started the preparations. She took off her clothes, felt the softness and calmness in her body as she walked around setting up the bath.

She lit some candles, started to fill the bathtub and heard the water softly running into the tub. It had to be hot, but not too hot, the steam was filling up the room. It was beautiful with the candles and the music. She felt so good.

Slowly she added the salt in the tub, then the crystals and lastly the oil. The smell of jasmine filled the room, it was dry, clean with hint of sweetness. She loved jasmine, the flower, the tea and now the oil.

Gently she climbed down into the tub. Started to relax, felt the hot water surrounding her skin, and the heat entering her bones. The water was completely still, she was playing with the surface of the water very slowly with her finger, watching the circles spread. Peace entered the room, the nipples just showing themselves of the surface of the still water.

"Ciao".

What was that? She looked around to see who was there. She couldn't see anything. *I must have heard it in my head.*
Then again...

"Ciao".

And then she saw him; in the air just in front of her a clear face was present. She had always known that the dead spirits were around her; she had never been interested in them and their shadows and had never seen anyone so clear, it was a holographic three dimensional person just in front of her.

She looked at him. Stunned. His face big and round in his twenties, dark hair. He looked at her. She looked at him.

"Who are you?"
"I'm Angelo Sebastinio".
"Luca's brother?"
"Si".

There was a long pause, she couldn't believe it, but for the first time in her life, she was aware that she wasn't afraid of this encounter. That made her curious.

"Why have you picked me?"
"Because I know you love Luca the same way I do and you would never try to own him!"
"Why are you here?"
"You have to tell Luca something".
"What do I have to tell him?"
"That you love him and that you're a gift to him".
"WHAT!"
"Are you crazy I don't want to do that. I don't want him to know that. He will misunderstand".
"You shouldn't be scared".
"But I am, and don't like it".
"Open up your heart, expand your heart".

When he said that, she felt Kim in her heart, she heard his voice, *Love, Love, Love, dare to love, open up, just be there with it.*

"I don't like it".
"I know. Tell him that I miss him and he shouldn't be scared anymore. I'm good".

"But will you come back?"

But it was to late he was gone. But his smiling eyes were etched into her memory.

She arose quickly from the bath. All wet, leaving lots of water on the floor, she found some paper and wrote all the information down. Tomorrow, she knew she had to tell Luca. They were going to meet. She knew within her heart that it would be difficult. She felt awful about it. Yet the experience was so real; she had no doubt that he had been there.

"Your face just crossed my heart – and my face lit up in a smile".

Katrin had packed her suitcase and was heading towards Luca. She was going directly to the airport after meeting him.

She was really nervous and thought of the sentence that had come to her, when thinking of her friend Luca at home. She was smiling to herself, it was a beautiful friendship and they had something very special. Now with Angelo suddenly being here, it somehow made more sense, why she felt the need to be around Luca.

She was sitting on the Metro, thinking. Soon she had to face him.

"Ciao, amica mia".
"Ciao".

She was aware she had closed in her energy; he looked at her, trying to figure out exactly what was wrong. But she knew that he had instantly realized something was not quite right.

They were talking about stuff, but she was not really present. Finally he said:

"What is it? Why are you so weird, you have been so unfocused all the time we have been speaking".

"I… I".

She stuttered and was looking down fumbling with the paper from last night.

"I took the bath last night, you know".

"Yes".

He smiled and watched her more intensely.

"Your brother came to me in the bath".

He looked at her with surprise, as if she had told him that she had become the new president. Something completely unbelievable.

She opened the paper.

"He had a message for you. He told me to tell you this.

He had chosen me because I love you the way he does, and I would never try to own you. He told me to tell you, that I'm a gift for you, and you should take it. He misses you, and you don't have to be scared anymore, he is good".

There was a period of silence. Luca folded his hands and covered his face, closed his eyes and took a deep breath.

139

"Yes that's him, he would never try to own anyone".

Luca looked up and looked her in the eyes.

"But we are not in love like that, we're friends".
"I know it is not like that".
"It's just love. Angelo know that it's not about trying to own you. It's the opposite".

How could she tell someone that this love had a different essence from what is normally described as love? She was on route to learn how to love unconditionally and now she had a new teacher, Angelo. Together with Kim, they taught her just to follow her heart.

Did she make a lot of mistakes?
Yes.
Did she fail to show unconditional love sometimes?
Sure.
But she tried.
Every day.
To become clearer.
To get wiser.
To learn from yesterday.
In the quest of learning
How to love.
Unconditionally.

"This is him".

Luca had taken his computer and showed her the photo of the real Angelo when he had been alive. She was so moved when she saw it. It was him she had seen.

They were both quiet.
They had to say goodbye.
She was late.
The flight was leaving.
They hugged.
He said "Ciao".
She said "Ciao".
Embarrassed.
Humble.
Sad.
Everything was
Awful.
The taxi came.
He put the suitcase in the back.
She left.
Sadness.
Silence
What was going on?

Why did she have to do such stupid things in life? And if she didn't, she knew she would pay back with her body stirring things up. She felt trapped within a souls journey and even if it was hers, she did not agree with the plan. She was angry, she was sad, why did she feel that she had to do it, when it only left her feeling so stupid? Like she didn't know anything about love.

She leaned back in the seat of the airplane, she was in the back row, luckily the seat next to her was empty. A man sat in the aisle seat. The tears started running down her cheeks, she put on her sunglasses.

"Are you okay?" The man looked at her.

"Are you scared of flying?"

"No, it's okay, thank you".

Katrin turned her head and looked away, watched the runway. The plane pushed back, let go and went into the skies, her tears wouldn't stop, and the pain wouldn't leave her. Why wouldn't it go away?

She was dozing off, when over the Alps she heard an Italian voice speaking to her. It was, as if she understood what he was saying to her even though it was in a language she did not know. She looked up; he was sitting right next to her. Talking and smiling at her.

She smiled, she couldn't answer him out loud on the plane but she suddenly knew, that she had gotten a new companionship in life. Right know it had the face of an Italian Angel. Angelo was a part of her life, and she had no control of when he was here, or at least that was her insight at this point.

She dozed off again, listening to him chatting and singing.

He was so happy that he had made contact with someone in an earthy body, one who loved his brother the same way he did.

It was indeed a splendid day for an angel.

"How did it go this time? Did you have a nice trip?"

Kim was curious about how her trip had gone. He saw her clumsiness, her intensity, and her attempt to learn how to love.

She told him the story about what had happened. He smiled.

"And Angelo knows that you're crazy enough to listen to him".
"Yes, I know, that's the beauty of me".

She laughed.
She felt she was on a right track.
That Angelo
Was a blessing.
A teacher.
Teaching her
To love.
Without receiving
Anything.
Just love.

It was time.
She laid herself down.
She relaxed.
Let go.
Fully.
Kim took her.
Her heart.
Her body.
He brought her to God.
She cried.
She just wanted to go home.
To God.
He held her.
Told her to feel the love.
In her heart.
Feel it.
Breath it.
Be it.
Be.
Love.

FOURTEEN

Why Rome?

Her days and flights to Rome became frequent. Always booking the next flight out when arriving home. The question kept looping in her mind.

"Why Rome? Why Rome? I want the answer; I don't know what I'm doing here. I know you match the inner feeling of my longing. It's like you have a piece of the puzzle to heal me. Maybe I don't get it, or maybe I'm just expecting that one day I will find the puzzle that fits. What can you teach me about love? The unsettling quest I have".

She knew that Luca and Angelo were a part of the whole learning process, but she didn't have the patience for it. Nor did she like the fact that two people seemed to be needed for her soul to heal. It wasn't nice to need, yet on a deeper level she realized we all required people for growth. But why?

She felt so stupid for being in love with Rome. All the time she received small signs that kept her going in her quest.

A vision came.
One morning
Waking up.
It was so clear.
A woman.
Old.
Living in a house.
In the penthouse.
With a view.
Of Rome.
Would have a key.
A gift.
For her.
It would be.
Important.
Soon.

Katrin had met a woman in Rome and they had become quite good friends, so every time she was in Rome she would meet up with her and they would go for a nice meal and good wines. They were almost name sisters. Caterina was this amazing artist who painted and was living in a little rustic loft space in Trastevere with her boyfriend. They had the most amazing time together, went for walks in Rome, visited all the churches lit candles and said prayers in every one. They had good talks about life and the quest of love. Caterina understood her, understood her pain, and often in the late evening they agreed, with too much wine in the blood, that it didn't matter. But then, when waking up in the morning the quest was still there.

Caterina had a grandmother whom she wanted Katrin to meet.

"You've got to meet my grandmother, you would love her. She has such a deep wisdom within her. She has been on many inner travels in her life and met a lot of great masters, maybe we should go there one day to have a cup of tea?"

"Yes that would be fantastic, next time I'm here we could go".

"Then we will do that my darling! when are you coming back?"

"In four weeks time".

"That's perfect. So what do you want to do tonight?"

"I thought we could go to that fantastic restaurant "Felice" you were talking about?"

"Yes perfect, I will call Alberto and some of his friends, then we could all hang out. But first I have to show you a secret place of Rome".

"I like that".

They took the bus from Piazza Argentina to Coliseum. Then they walked a bit up a little road just near Coliseum. She was amazed, that if you just walked to the opposite side of Coliseum, there were no tourists or at least very few. You got to the private part of Rome.

"Where are you taking me?"

Caterina was laughing.

"You will see, it's a little treasure of Rome, not many know this. Ahhh…. see here, there it is, Basilica of San Clemente, a beautiful church with a nice surprise".

They went into the church and lit a candle, and then they went and bought a ticket. There was a part of the church that had an ancient history. They went inside the door and walked down. Underneath were buildings in two layers, the first one was an old Mithraeum, a kind of temple, and then below that a house from a nobleman. It was amazing, first the church and then hidden from view all this history. They went into a room in the lower basement, a special dark room, where the waters of Rome run through. They sat down, closed their eyes and listened to the sound of running water. The purest of Rome, found in a secret little room of an old home.

"God you're amazing Caterina, you just know all the small bits of Rome. Thank you so much. I love it".

"It's my grandmother, she knows everything about Rome. That's why I wanted to take you here, because I know that my grandmother would love that you have been here to see it".

Caterina smiled.
She smiled back.
She knew
That Caterina
Had just taken her
To a place where
She would
Be closer
To that
Part of her
That longed
To be
Healed.
She
Knew

Intuitively.
What she needed
To heal.
That part
Of herself
That was longing
Back
Into the Roman
Blood.
Every time:
Caterina
Was so
Right.

"You should go to this street tomorrow if you want to, it's just a little further away from Coliseum. I promise you, it's spectacular."

"And I promise that I will go".

Smiles again.
Understanding.
Loving.
Rome.
It was
A mess.
A wonderful mess.
Some days.
A deep breath
Of Rome
Was in her lungs.
The lungs of her soul.
Breathing in.
That part

She felt was
So strongly
Missed.

The next day she went to the street Caterina had talked about. She had just taken a walk in the center of Rome and had gotten her favorite ice cream at Giolitti's and then walked all the way out to this special street. It was just on the right, off from very heavy traffic, and then it was completely quiet. It was a street paved with just cobblestones. No traffic at all. She started to walk, she could sense green areas on both sides, and small parks she guessed. There was a huge old brick wall on either side. She walked slowly; a little bit puzzled why Caterina had said it was a remarkable street. She felt it was quite boring. Then suddenly, she could hear horses and a sense of days gone past, like a three dimensional picture with small market places it was alive in front of her. She could see a thief. Then in a split second a huge amount of cars came driving at very high speed down the road. And then again in a split second, they were all gone. Suddenly the three dimensional picture was back, warriors were in the street, fights were going on, and then once more it was all gone and the traffic came back.

She was trying to move forward but her legs would not move, she turned around and ran. When she arrived at the hectic traffic road again, life returned to normal, she looked back and felt she had just been in a time machine. It was the strangest thing she had ever experienced.

"What is it with Rome? What are you doing to me? Let me be done!"

One month had passed, she had talked to Caterina, she had laughed, she knew the secret about the street. She didn't always get her humor. But now afterwards, maybe it was kind of funny.

They met at the metro station Cavour.

"Sooooo good to see you my love, I missed you so. How was your flight?"

"It was up and down, really easy. And yes me too, it's so good to see you. I can't wait to see your grandmother. I'm really looking forward to meeting her".

"She looks forward to it too… Any news from the angel?"

Caterina smiled and winked.

"Yes he is there all the time, but right now I don't want to talk to you about that. I'll tell you next time we met. What is your grandmother's name?

"It's Maria".

"And where does she live?"

"Not so far, just near by the church Santa Maria Maggiore".

"Nice, I'm so looking forward to see her".

They got to the building, pressed the button.

The door opened, they went in and took the lift to the top floor.

Maria opened the door and the stairs led to the most amazing apartment she had ever seen. A huge loft space with two big balconies and a view of Rome that was priceless. It was a magnificent place. She walked around hearing Caterina and Maria chit chatting in the background. Absorbing the whole place.

They sat down at a table and Maria looked her straight in the eyes, she didn't say anything. She knew that she saw her soul; she knew Maria was looking deep within her.

"I knew you were coming my dear".

She smiled a secret smile at her, with her deep penetrating eyes.

At that moment.
She saw
That Maria
Was the woman
She had seen
coming.
That
She
Was
Important
To her life.
To her journey.

She knew a new part of the journey had started; that Maria was a gift and she would spend time with her.

It was a wonderful afternoon; she could hear that Maria was a wise woman. She listed to her, only replying when asked, felt the humbleness of the situation.

When she got home. Maria called her and said.

"I think I love you".

Why Rome?
Why Rome?
Why you?
What do you
Have to tell me?
I feel you own me.
By my fascination.
By my love
For you.
Like me being it all.
The nun.
The Italian.
The whore.
The passionate.
The crazy one.
The angel.
The church.
The food.
The lover.
The crazy car driver.
Coffee lover.
She kept wondering.
Kept asking.
Rome.
Question.
The only thing.
That came
Back
Was
Silence
And
A heart

Longing
To come
Home and
Understand
What it was
All about.

FIFTHTEEN

The Choice

The days had changed; Angelo had become a part of them. He came, he went and she had welcomed it. He had been in the car when she arrived home from Rome. Suddenly laughing out loud, lots of Italian words. He was like a child, a young child. Turning up the music. It made her laugh. She was aware that she needed to be careful not to let people see her appearing to be talking to herself or responding to something that was not to be seen by anyone else other than Katrin.

He made her go and put on some music one day. He wanted her specifically to choose an opera singer, Andrea Bocelli, singing Con Te Partiró. They played it really loud singing in Italian, laughing and dancing. He constantly disturbed her, like a child constantly wanting to be entertained. He was so heartfelt; a deep vibrant energy surrounded him. He had this openhearted, naive yet very intelligent energy about him, you could feel his open approach to life, but it just added more love to the whole relationship. Slowly she fell in love with him, loved that he was there, loved his spirit.

She also felt stuck between two brothers. She didn't know how to handle it. How to be respectful towards the both of them.

She had booked a trip to Thailand, she was going to a retreat center. She had heard of a special person who could help her understand how to receive these angels, so she went.

Life had gotten a new dimension.
It felt so normal.
Like it should be.
That he.
Angelo
Was here.
She had asked him
Not to
Be around
All of the time.
She felt bad
Like a child.
Only to want
Him,
When she wanted him.
How could she
Feel peace
With it?
Thailand
A possible
Opening.
Didn't know
What to expect?

Just the hope that
Clarity
Of the situation
Would enter into her life.

She was going with a whole group to Thailand. They were 12. She quickly connected with one woman; the conversation was open and personal in a few seconds. They had a coffee before boarding. They flew directly to Bangkok and then they had a 1-1/2 hours bus ride to the beautiful resort where they were going to be for a week.

She got a room with her new friend Marian. A beautiful room with a huge bamboo bed in the middle, orchids everywhere, dark red walls, huge windows with a view on the mountains surrounding the place, buddha sculptures and a smell of the soft sandlewood incense that had been burned.

"God this is nice, did you see the pool?"

"Yes it's amazing and the massage room with a view of the hills. I can't wait to get my massage?"

"Me neither".

They were unpacking their bags, settling-in, tired from the trip, excited and exhausted.

Katrin found a chair outside, found her inner peace, reflected. Life felt like a mess. A mess with an angel. Love, damn it was difficult. What was it all about? She couldn't really get it. Could she learn how to love without the need to process or even be physically near a man, but just love for no reason? She had seen this inner picture of a man and a woman melting together. Was it possible to meet that man she could melt with? Or was it just a metaphor for healing? She felt both.

And now she was stuck in-between two brothers. She loved them both, but it felt so daunting, so heavy. She hoped the searching and learning would end soon. Always that damn impatience.

They all met for dinner. The freshness of a new group was still in the air. The excitement and joy of being here. For some, it was the first time ever that they had given them self space for a deeper view within and for others it was a part of their on-going journey through life.

She and Marian went for a late walk. Listing to the silence of Thailand, the evening sounds from the animals and the energy from the hills. They already knew quite a lot about them self which was why they both had chosen to come here. Marian had been really sick from stress and was still recovering, trying to find a new path in life.

"Why did you come all the way to see this woman? Aren't there any others in Denmark or Europe?"

"Yes there might be, but sometimes I just know within that it's not just a person, but it's the whole trip around it that is healing too. So already you have entered my life and all the healing the group will do together is a part of my healing and the groups healing. So it's not just one person. Does that make sense?"

"Yes I understand now, otherwise it could seem a little overwhelming, but maybe it's me that feels that everything is a bit overwhelming. When are you going to see her?"

"In two days. She doesn't live that far away from here, so I can take a taxi to her place".

"That's nice. What do you hope for?"

"I don't quite know. I hope that she can help me to feel peace because I feel trapped between the two, Angelo and

Luca. And I'm not sure whether Luca actually likes it. I don't quite know what it's all about. I'm confused. I am trying to do the right thing I surpose, but I don't really know what the right thing is. Maybe she can help me with that".

The day had come.
She was on her own.
Just for a while.
This was
The actual
Reason
That she
Was here.
To
Tell
To
Listen
To
This woman.
The woman knew
When souls
Were attaching
To your life.
What to do with it!
How to be!
How to choose!
She didn't
Know
That she had this
Choice.
And often felt…

Do we
Actually have a
Choice?

She had been wondering for a long time, whether or not she really did have a choice in life. She often felt a strong will, as if it was not hers, choosing the way for her. She silently felt that others who didn't have to listen to their soul and body as much were in luck. She felt that she didn't have a choice. In a way she knew she did, but often something greater in her always won the game, but wasn't that in a way her choice as well? She hadn't made peace with that one yet. She felt that she followed her heart and somehow that felt like a nicer approach to it all.

The taxi driver had come just in time; he knew were she was going and they went in silence. She noticed that once in a while he watched her in the rear view mirror. She pretended to be in her own world looking out the window. The landscape was beautiful, rice fields everywhere, green, it was so green right here. There was a smell of cooked rice and heat. The wind made a soft movement in her hair. She felt free and at peace for a moment.

"Ciao".
"Ciao, Bello".
"How are you my dear".
"Wonderful".

He was sitting next to her in the taxi now. She was carefully looking at the taxi driver, watching him. She didn't want him to think she was crazy. She had picked up her phone so it looked like she was speaking on the phone. Clever move she thought. Angelo was in a sparkling mood. Enjoying the fact that she was going to see a woman whom she could talk to about him.

"What do you want to know?"
"I don't' know yet, but you've got to let me do this. Stay out, when I'm talking to her – okay?"

He didn't answer but continued.

"It's such a stupid song they are playing on the radio".
"What?"
"Yes, I like Italian music better, ciao ciao!"

He was gone. She looked at the phone as if it has been cut off. This was so annoying about him, he sometimes just showed up like this all over the place. This was exactly the thing she felt was disturbing.

Katrin arrived at the house, paid the taxi driver. She was way out in the countryside of Thailand. The house had a nice spirit, she could tell, the house was practically glowing, there was a calmness surrounding it. It was tiny and sweet. She went to the door and knocked. She could hear slow steps moving forward towards the door.

The door opened and a warm smile and intense look greeted her. She was short and had a long warm red dress on. She had the most beautiful brown eyes, with a sparkling twist.

"Hello my friend".
"Hello, thank you for meeting me".
"What are you here to tell me?"

"I have a very dear friend whom I have a very special love for, and his brother who is dead comes to me often with messages. I don't know how to handle this. I feel I'm caught in-between, I'm not sure that my friend is interested in hearing the messages that I get for him, but at the same time I feel that I have to pass them on. That it's my path, I feel stuck yet I feel I have a lesson to learn as I, myself, have a deep pain".

She paused, feeling the tears pressing from the inside trying to get out. Looking up. She saw that this woman had an understanding even if she hadn't spoken yet.

"You are right. You have a lesson to learn. He is showing up to teach you just to love with no agendas. But you know that right?"

"Yes I do".

"Then what is it? You do know that you have the right to tell him that he shouldn't be here right?"

"No I didn't, I thought his agenda was greater than mine".

"Dearest it's always your choice. Never forget that. But if you feel that you have a greater lesson to learn here, then you can decide to embrace it. You do have a choice".

Katrin's tears were silently running now. Looking up. Not really sure what it all meant. Why was she sad that she could choose to ask the angel to leave?

"I just realized that I don't want him to leave yet, only if I'm not the right person for Luca…"

"You are doing something really beautiful, don't forget that, but don't forget yourself."

"Thank you, I'm very grateful. Thank you for your time".

"That's the least I can do".

Katrin left. Headed back to the hotel. Feeling relieved and sad, she knew that she had to talk to Angelo so he could choose someone else to pass on the messages to Luca. Love was not about attaching but letting go so that the other person's life would expand and they would become more. She didn't want to be the one in the middle preventing that growth.

She was so tired that evening. She cried in silence so Marian wouldn't hear her. She couldn't sleep, she was torn apart by the feeling that Luca might not be interested in receiving the messages from Angelo. It was as if he wanted her to learn how to love actively. Using her heart instead of talking about opening up. The wilderness within, the sorrow, the pain, the woman's words. She didn't feel she could let go of him; she didn't feel it was her choice, not yet. Something bigger in life wanted her to do differently. Who's voice was that? Some might say it was her heart, some might say it was God, the universe, but really it didn't matter. Something inside of her was just not able to tell Anglo to go away.

Her tears,
Were running
Down her
Cheeks.
Tucking in
Curling up
Her
Body
Was
Sad,
Very sad.
She felt,
Him

Before
She saw him.
Angelo.
Looking at
Her
Touching
Her face.
He held her
With
His
Arms.
Holding her.
The silence.
Warmness
Of his
Heart
Touched
Her deep within.

"Please let me go. If I'm not the right one, then please let me go. Go to someone who Luca would listen to, it's okay that it's not me. He is more important in this matter. Go to his wife if she is closer".

"But you know I can't do that. You're the only one loving him and never wanting to own him at the same time".

"Yes but I feel trapped here. Like a fool".

"But we are fools when we love…"

"I don't like looking like a fool. I don't know if I am doing it the right way".

"There is no right way, only your way. And yes, I will let you go, if you really want to, but think about it. Give it time. Grow with it. Grow with your heart. Love… always love".

She cried some more. He held her. He showed her a memory of when Luca was seven, sitting by his desk in Pitigliano writing, writing about life.

"Tell Luca that he has it all in him. Tell him to let it out".
"I will".

She
Gave in.
Her body
Sank into
His body.
Letting
The night
Of Thailand.
Into the arms
Of an angel.
Taking her
Away.

SIXTEEN

A Crystal Of Heart

She met Caterina the next time she was in Rome. Caterina came on her scooter. She had been so kind to pick her up at the main train station.

"Ciao Bella. Hop on, and take this helmet".

"Ciao Bello. Come stai? Do you really want me to do this?"

"Bene, Bene and Yes, sure".

"Were are we going?"

"You will see, it's beautiful my friend, you will see".

"Nice".

"Are you hungry? We could grab a bite before going".

"Yes, that would be so good. Let's go".

Caterina made a huge swing. She hung on to her, breathing deep, telling herself that everything was okay and she was not going to die now. The fear of the traffic was a bit intimidating to her body, but breathing could do it.

> The warm wind
> In Rome
> Touched
> Her skin.
> Letting go
> Of thoughts
> Emotions.
> On a
> Scooter
> With
> A beautiful
> Friend.
> Noise.
> Lust.
> Coffee.
> People.
> Italians.
> Words.
> Mess.
> Beauty.
> People.
> She was
> Back
> In her
> Center.

Caterina stopped the scooter, took off her helmet and smiled at her.

"Here we are! Let's have some food. What do you want? They have the most crispy pizza here".

"Sounds great, let me have two slices and a coke!"

"What slice?"

"Just any of your choice, you know the best ones".

Katrin found a table for them outside and waited for Caterina to bring the food. As always she was in heaven just being here.

"So Bella, you never told me about the angel, last time you were here. By the way, I should tell you hi from my grandmother".

"Thanks, well…"

"I mean, what is going on? How does Luca take it? And why in God's name is this happening?"

Caterina was half eating, talking and laughing. She was so full of life that woman. Katrin loved her.

"Well so many things are happening all the time. I have just been on a retreat in Thailand and I met this amazing elderly woman… And he is coming all the time in a different version… and I'm not sure Luca likes it… but I still feel like…"

Caterina cut her off.

"Sweetheart could you take it from the beginning, could you just tell me what is going on? I don't understand anything at all".

"Yes sure, but it's just so much".

"I understand".

Silence.

"Well you know, Angelo came to me in the bath and I got so upset and sad that I had to tell Luca, right?"

"Yes, and I also know that he came to you at home in the car, but what then? What do you think he wants?"

"Well, it feels like he is here for three reasons. Sometimes he is coming with God, like a divine energy from a higher source to show me how to love unconditionally, and Luca is the one to "practice" on. Other times he is wise in life, a brother loving his brother and wanting to tell him that everything is good. That he misses him and wishes to give him hints on how to live his life. And then he is sometimes just like a very small child showing his beautiful traits, dancing, laughing and enjoying life. I never know what is coming".

"But how do you see him?"

"I can see him like a three dimensional holographic structure. It's very real. And Luca showed me a picture of him. It is really him. It's amazing. But I feel so stuck with it sometimes... I went to Thailand as I told you and I met this woman and she said that it was my choice if I wanted him around, but she also confirmed that I had some learning to do, so in a way I don't quite feel that I have a choice..."

"Yes I know what you mean, even if we have a free choice it also feels like we have to go through so many experiences sometimes. That we don't have a choice".

"Yes exactly, that's it".

"So what do you want to do?"

"Well... I'm very aware of the learning part, and that is the part that I hate the most. It makes me vulnerable, and I don't like to be. At the same time I feel it's just exactly what I need to ease my pain. I know it".

"You're amazing. I really think you are and you are doing such a wonderful healing".

They smiled to each other. No more words were needed. They went to visit friends by the sea. They had wine and dinner. She got pissed. Got home. Took a shower. Masturbated. Felt the ease in her body. Fell asleep.

She woke up in the night.
Angelo
The angel
He came
He showed his face.
He was there
With
God.
Asking her
To Love
Luca.
Turning her heart
In his direction.
Opening up
To
Him and God.
Her heart
Full of
Love.
She had
Cried.
Her heart
Was in
Pain.

"What is it with the pain? I have to open up to it, embrace it. Feel it. I know the love to Luca can heal it. But why is it so hard to love. It's like reaching out for something bigger and Angelo is showing

me that space. It's really beautiful. So, why the pain? Love, love, love. I know it's the answer – I hear you Kim, I hear you Angelo"

She fell asleep with a smile on her face. She had two very beautiful hearts showing her how to love without the need to get anything back. Just the pure energy of love; It would be better. Soon.

Luca called the next day. Telling her that his mom Celia was going to the hospital to have heart surgery. Katrin calmed him down and they talked about his mom. He told her how wonderful she was, what she was like, and when hearing about her, she immediately felt a strong connecting to her. Luca was really scared that something bad would happen to her during the surgery, but it helped talking about it.

They hung up. Only two seconds after Angelo was there in his cheeky spirit.

"Mom is going to surgery".

"Yes I know. Luca just told me".

"I'm going to stay with her, when she is in".

"That sounds wonderful".

"Yes, she will be happy to see me. Also you have to buy Luca a crystal".

"What do you mean?"

"Yes you have to buy him a crystal from me. You will know which one to buy".

"But…?"

But he was already gone.

Mad angel she thought to herself. Feeling even weirder herself for listing to him. She took the car and drove all the way down to the crystal shop where she had bought the very crystals that she needed for the bath where she met Angelo the first time.

She went in, walked around in the shop. Crystals were not her favorite thing, but anyway. She looked at them all, she felt that it had to be a specific size. She knew exactly when she found it, picked it up. It was beautiful. She paid and left.

Katrin was going to meet Luca in the afternoon. She drove to the sea, took a walk on the beach, felt the sand, and breathed in the Roman air, listened to the heartbeat of the sea. She felt happy. More than she had been in a long time. It was as if her pain would vanish for brief moments. Still time to go, but slowly Rome was healing her. As if Rome knew her soul and what she needed.

She met Luca at a café. He had ordered two glasses of wine. It was a nice Italian square with a lot of life.

"Ciao, Good to see you".
"Good to see you too".
"How is life?"
"It's good. I feel it's getting better and better. I just thought about it by the sea, how thing are getting easier and easier".
"It's Rome".
"I know, I know".

She smiled – he smiled. She felt the usual unease when doing this.

"He's been here again".
"Who".
"Your brother".

"Ah, so what's up this time?"

"Well he asked me to buy you a crystal, so I went to buy one for you".

She gave him the crystal, feeling utterly stupid.

"Wow, Grazie!"

He took the crystal. Genuinely happy with it. She was a bit surprised that he was so happy about the crystal, and felt more relaxed than she had ever been about passing on a message to him. Maybe he wasn't as reluctant about the messages as she thought?

"Wow, have you seen it?"

"What do you mean?"

"Look… it looks like a heart".

He turned the crystal around and she could see it, she had bought a crystal in the shape of heart. She was amazed, a coincidence? Maybe not.

Luca smiled. His phone rang. Celia was calling to tell that the surgery went well and all was good. He was relieved. She also told him that Angelo had been there, to visit her, when she had been in surgery. Once again the magic angel had been around, just as he said he would.

She smiled.
Felt all
The love
Between brothers
Mother and sons.

172

She was
A part
A silent
Part.
She felt
Humble
That he had
Chosen her.
That she was
The eye
The translator
For a love
That was
Greater
Than life.
The lesson
Of love
Is never a
Simple one.

SEVENTEEN

What Is Love?

In the quest for love, to relieve the pain in her soul her travels had become many.–One part consisted of her travels and the angel, the other side of it was the understanding of love. She felt lost in the sense of what love was. She had received all these beautiful helpers on her way, they were her outer mirrors. Why did it have to be about being together with someone in order to justify that you loved him or her? Couldn't you just love someone and feel that they were a part of your journey? Or was it really a necessity to have a fully committed relationship to love completely? That was not how she felt. But her mind didn't understand what the heart did. The feeling of love sent by Angelo through her heart was like a big pile of love energy opening it up towards Luca, with no fear, no attachment, no agenda. It was greater that anything she had ever received before, and Kim was teaching her to feel and obtain it in her body. Not to be scared of it, not to be scared of loving for no reason. She did a lot of reflection upon all the obstacles that she felt within. What was to be learned?

Love
You are such a pure
Energy.
Who are you?
What do you want?
How to express
You?
Is it the silence?
Do I
Have
To communicate you?
Do I
Have
To live you?
How can I not?
When you
In every
Moment
Demand
Me to
Be with you.
Do I fail?
In love
When I
Don't know
How to?
Or is it the
You calling
Me to be
You?

Katrin had many good conversations with Kim. About the frustration of love, the sorrow of feeling that she had to love someone and not be their partner, but to solely open up the heart. She knew that Luca was a part of this journey; it was just really hard to be in that tension. But she also knew that the tension was the answer. Breathing in the pain and then transforming it by loving it. She felt like she just had to be around her friend Luca. The journey with him, the small talks and being in Rome would heal her, she knew.

She was going to meet Luca again. They were often going for rides in his car and they always had really good talks about life. Every time they were together it felt like it was of high importance. Like when a seed of a pomegranate was leaving its shelve with a richness to dive within. They were processing a lot together; honesty and insights were just as common as a cup of coffee.

"Ciao Bella".

"Ciao Bello".

"Come stai?"

"Crap. I feel like crap".

"Yes me too".

"Where are we going?"

"We are going to a meditation just outside Rome, near the sea. It should be a fantastic place".

"I'm very much looking forward to that. So why are you feeling like crap?"

"Just life, I can't wrap my head around it. So many things are not falling into place".

"Yes I know what you mean, it's the same here".

They left central Rome and headed outside the city up north following the coast. Their conversations very intimate and deep, neither one of them ever satisfied with just scratching the surface.

"I miss him. I miss Angelo so much. I can hardly breath sometimes. No one will ever understand my pain".
"Yes, it's impossible to understand someone else's pain. It's so personal…"
"I miss you too".

Her words left her mouth in an almost whispering sound. She sometimes didn't know how the words just slipped out of her mouth. It was as if Angelo's words had just bypassed her conscience.

"Shit, I shouldn't have said that. Where does it come from? Is this when the heart is just talking and there are no filters?"

He looked at her. She could see his sorrow and his gentle surprise by her words.

"Sorry. I didn't mean to hurt you. I don't know were it's coming from"
"You didn't hurt me".

The silence between them was so intense now; both just starring at the road.
From the silence her lips slowly formed words.

"I sometimes wonder if you want to get these message, I mean I don't want to hurt you and I don't know why he is here. I can't turn him away. I think it's difficult. Do you want the messages?"

She held her breath. The silence again, so intense. Packed in the car like a heavy cloud.

"How could I not want them?"

"I don't know. It's just so difficult to bring them to you".

"I know. But he has come before to other people also. He came to me too the day he died. He had said that he would always be here, that I should be strong and that he would always love me. And I just feel such a failure, because I never feel strong anymore. I feel so empty without him. He was my gold, my inner gold".

Luca's face was like a stone now. Holding back the pain. She could never take away his sorrow but she could offer him her silent presence.

"Come let's get an ice cream. I need a rest".

They bought the ice cream and sat down in the shade. It was a hot day.

"Why do you think that he is coming to me?"

"I don't know. It's hard to tell. He was loved by everyone and had so much life. I can't understand why God took him away from us".

"No it doesn't make sense. It's the hardest part in life when something doesn't make sense I think".

"Yes, I agree… you have some kind of excuse for it to happen if you find meaning in it. It's harder to think that many things happen for no reason and you don't understand it."

"Mmmm I feel the same. It's better to become aware, but it's also a job I would like to quit. I wish I could be the postman, not wanting to understand. I know a postman would be able to understand too, but you get the picture. Why did I choose to search and what is the search about? It just feels like a burden and excuse not to live a real life. Maybe the postman is wiser".

She smiled and they laughed. It was a question with no answer. Sometimes the most simple man or woman could be the one holding on to the greatest source of wisdom, and now she was searching and travelling in order to get wisdom.

They drove some more and all of a sudden a huge argument about living a true life developed between them. Something had sparked them off, their pain and confusion had collided in each other's interpretation of the way they saw the world.

They arrived at the house were the meditation was taking place. It was on a terrace by the sea and the evening was pure magic.

The meditation began and she glanced over the whole group. They were fifty. The teacher asked them to close their eyes and enter their center. She followed the directions of the teacher to one point, then it all became blurred and her heart entered her mind. Her heart in its presence cleaned up the bits that prevented her from feeling the truth of her heart.

The heart
Again
Felt so strong.
She
Could

See it
Hear it
Taste it
Feel it
So present.
Beating away
Like
Nothing could
Stop it.
So excited
To be alive.
To live.
To love.
Getting closer
To her own
Heart
Was so
Amazing.
She felt she
Was getting closer.
To the end
Of the pain.

The sun had almost left the day. The darkness of the night had entered and the feeling of the event closing down on the roof had a clean and uplifting spirit. Everything felt so fresh and new. They hugged everyone, saying goodbye. Heard some wonderful music on the way home.

She entered her room, tired and happy. Her heart, she felt it, what a wonderful center she had.

The next day she went to see Maria Caterina's grandmother. She had come here regularly since they first met; she felt that she had something for her. A present like she had seen in the vision. They would talk about art and life. Maria was certainly a very wise woman.

"Ciao".

"Ciao, I love to be here with you. It's the best".

"Do you want tea?"

"Yes please that would be really nice".

"How have you been my dear? May I see you?"

"I'm better, I'm getting much better all the time. I had a beautiful meditation yesterday by the sea. I got home to my heart. It was amazing".

"I can see that. You are getting more and more clean my dear. Let's sit on the terrace".

She told Maria about what was happening inside her. Maria loved to hear about her unfolding of herself. She always had small comments and direction but never an answer.

Over the time she had understood that Maria didn't have a specific present. Maria was the present. One day she had taken her hands in hers and told her the wisdom of the hands. Their signature was how open they were to receive and give love. She had burst into tears when Maria's hand had opened hers. The pain of feeling how restricted she really was.

Maria hugged her very tight when she left. She felt that she had been given an Italian grandmother. It was special.

What is love?
This wonderful
Concept

That fills our life
In the joy
In the sadness
In the darkness
In the light.
The energy
That is always there.
You just
Have to
Take off your
Glasses.
Depending on the
Mud.
Depending on
Your filter
Is how hard
It is
For you
To
Love.

EIGHTEEN

The Letting Go

Despite all the beautiful people she was meeting in Rome and all the insights she was getting, she still always wanted to leave Rome. Rome had become a symbol of finishing this pain and she had made up the equation, that when she was done in Rome she would be done with her pain. This was an ever-present thought of hers. The need for Rome was the need for her soul to heal.

The spinning of thoughts never came to a rest. She longed for some reprieve but got scared when she felt it. Thought some more because she wanted to figure out the meaning of it all. The feeling of being fucked-up had vanished, now there was a need to finish. Time in Rome was undoubtedly healing her. But she was still waiting for the time to let go and be set free.

Katrin spent many days walking around in Rome, just being with it. Drinking cappuccinos, reading, walking with her reflections on love. The feeling of wanting to reach out for the essence of love, was helped along by Angelo, there was no doubt. He was showing her the essence of loving. How the heart was vibrating when you loved, the true feelings when you really experience love. She felt a deep longing to share this love that she was learning with someone. Not Luca, but someone whom she could share this new awareness of love with. She was ready to go, but knew that it was not yet time.

She was sitting one night in her room. Crying out for an answer, the decision was clear she wanted to leave even though the time was not ready yet. She couldn't handle the struggle anymore.

"I'm done with Rome, no matter what, enough is enough. I don't know what I'm doing here anymore. I constantly walk around, trying to find the answer written behind a secret stone".

Rome!
I'm done.
Done with you.
Done with this.
Can't find
The meaning
Of you.
How
Can
I be
So angry with
You
When you're
So beautiful?
Why Can't
I

Find
The final
Answers
Within?
Set me
Free.
I want
To let
Go...

She could hear herself and how stupid it all sounded. She wanted a city to set her free so she could let go... But she didn't care, even if from deep within she had a knowing she couldn't leave, she decided to pack her stuff and leave anyway.

Katrin sat by the desk in her room, the room was full of candles and the sweet rose smell from burning incense. She was in her world of thoughts, the ones that kept looping around, constantly trying to solve it.

"I have got to leave, what am I doing here? It doesn't make sense, and no matter how hard I try, I can't get the final piece in place. I want to go!!!"

"Please don't".

"What? Ah... it's you, Angelo".

"Why can't I leave?"

"Please I beg of you?"

"But why? I'm clearly not getting the point! I'm not getting through to Luca, it's like he doesn't quite want me to give him the messages and being around like this as a friend is a beautiful gesture. But in a way I feel I would rather spend the time with someone that I should be with. At the same time, I know that I'm learning to simply love, to give love, be love.

But I feel like I'm so bad at it. It's like I still expect something from it. A result and even then, it's like I don't mind letting go of the expectation too. But why? What is it?"

"Please I beg you, I know what you are going through. I know it's hard to love just for that, but you have asked for the trip, you know it's your soul's longing to get home, and this is your journey".

"But why do you want me to stay around to love your brother. Why? I don't understand – to some point yes, but for a lot of reasons no. And I know I'm not ready to let you go yet. You know that. Why is that so?"

"You just have to stay, you have to find it within you. But please stay, stay in Rome some more".

She was laughing and crying at the same time.

"It's impossible to say no to you. I love you my Italian Angel. I really do".

"I know".

"But it's not about us being a couple right? Luca and I, because I don't want that".

"No, No, No Bella".

They were laughing together. They both knew that this was a hilarious picture.

"No, but just stay!"

"I will, I promise you. For now".

"God I must be crazy to listen to an angel. Why am I feeling that this is so important? I wish that I had a normal reason for doing this. Is this what happens when you listen to your heart? Doing things that make no sense and still knowing that it's

important? Maybe it's not so much about whom and how I love; maybe it is about me following that voice within that is the greatest source of love. This is where I get close to the abundance flow, the energy that is called Love. From there it's all about the sharing with the ones that are given to you".

She loved
An angel.
Her Italian angel.
He spread
Joy
Challenges
Wisdom
And an opening
That she
Would not
Have chosen
If she had
Decided
For herself.
He came
To nourish
And guide
Her
So her
Heart would
Open.

After he had left, she sat for a while starring, trying to grasp what had happened once again. That he came, shared, asked, and showed her his heart. She couldn't believe it. Just as she thought that she could call it off, he came, as she wanted to go.

Katrin went to see Maria the next day. She was confused about it all. She had told Maria the story about Luca and Angelo and she had listened to her, no advice given, she had simply been there to hear her story.

"I just want it to be over. But something inside me can't let go of him yet".

"When you can't let go, it's because you are not done. Why the rush?"

"I want get away from this absurd situation. An angel is telling me that I have to stay around his brother, and I guess I feel it's such an intimidating situation. I feel I'm in the middle of a broken love between brothers and it's not mine to fix, and then he is showing all this wonderful energy..."

"Why do you really think that he had chosen you? If you are just completely honest with yourself".

"Do you want me to answer now?"

"Whenever. There is no rush, it's more important that you find the answer yourself. No one in the world can tell you that".

"I guess I know. I'm just always hoping that someone can tell me what it's all about. Like I need to do it in a certain way or learn a specific lesson, otherwise I have to stay in this".

"Dearest, there is no right or wrong way. It's only you – and just you who can receive that wisdom".

"I know somehow. But I'm scared that I will never get it".

"You will, you are too honest and too strong a soul to never receive that wisdom from within, but you have a huge challenge and that is your patience and the need to get a result. Not many are able to experience what you are, and you want to throw it away. Why? This is your gift; receive it with your heart. It's not the result that matters; it's your perception of it - your learning".

"I guess, I'm just so tired of learning. I want to share love".

"I understand my dear and sometimes when we're in touch with a pain like yours, there is no other thing to do, than follow the uncertain path and open up to all the hearts that are joining you on your way to come back to you. It's a lonely trip, but you're not alone, and love is all around. You know that".

"Yes I do. And I also feel that the quest of love is a fine balance between the divine and earth. To bring it into action. I see that more and more, and the conflict of bringing Angelo's messages to Luca is a very special picture of it. Realizing the vulnerability in bringing them to him is my special gift to open up my heart. To just do whatever my heart tells me to".

"Yes and we always think that it ought to be in a different way than the reality is showing us. Often we are too scared to go with the heart, but you're really doing it, even if it's very different from what most people experience. Be proud of that and be proud of how far you have come. It's not always easy, I know".

"Thank you... I guess I just feel that I'm not really as pure as I could be because a little part of me also wanted to romantically be with Luca, so the love is a little muddled as I also have to learn from him as well."

"You are human, never forget that. We humans tend to think, that if we could be the divine love, all would be good. But it's not until we bring that love down and share it with someone else, that we actually fully feel it. It seems like this is what happened to you and that you're having a very exceptional journey in all of this. Remember that you are only given this challenge because you can solve it".

"Thank you".

"Maybe it's time you tell Luca everything and then let it go. Maybe this is the last piece. I think your heart knows this but you are afraid to leave and fully let go? Or I could be wrong".

"Yes I know, but I got confused because Angelo came again and asked me to stay and I felt compelled to do that, because I didn't felt ready yet to let go fully. But still that was yesterday, now it's today. I'm going home tomorrow. I will know what to do next time I see Luca. I need to make sure that I let go properly, maybe that's why he came, he gave me some extra time?"

She smiled to Maria and Maria smiled back. She surely was a gift in her life, that dear Maria.

The engines start.
The plane
Warms up
Slowly.
Moving to the
Runway.
Engines are
Spinning.
Pulling back.
Setting free.
Letting go
From the
Roman ground
To fly.
With such
A question
In mind
So big.
What will it
Take to

Fully
Let go?

She knew that next time in Rome would be different, she could just feel the change deep within.

She had decided to see Kim, she had to be fully integrated with herself for the last stretch of the journey. It was time to let go. The time at home after her visit to Maria had made it clear. She was getting ready to face it.

"It was so strange the last time I was there. Angelo came and asked me to stay, but I just can't anymore. I'm tired of being the messenger and I'm not sure that Luca is benefitting from it at all".

"Let go, it's not your job, don't stay and love when there is no receiver anymore".

"I guess you are right. I have loved and loved all the time as you said, but it's like there is nothing more left, just peace".

Kim had helped her body process it all and to open up her heart, cleanse and love. Today had been no exception and the body was ready too. She could feel it so intensely in every cell, the love, and the joy of being human, close to God, close to her heart and close to love. It was all there. It was time to meet Luca and say goodbye.

She was back in Rome. It was time to see Luca. She had called him and they were going to go for a ride in the car to the coast up north. There was a little church he had always wanted to show her so they were going there. She glanced at him in the car while driving. They kept silent for a long time, just staying in their own thoughts.

Katrin broke the silence.

"I have been thinking a lot about love... the whole thing about following your heart... you know that!"
"Yes I do".

He glanced at her and turned off the music.

"... And I have been thinking a lot about why Angelo had come to me. Why he is here. He clearly misses you and I have had a lot of learning to do. But I also feel that it's time for me to let go now. How do you feel about that?"

He went very quiet and she hated that, when he was silent in a special way it was because he was not happy about it. She knew that she was looking for the truth within her right now, and she knew it made her really annoying because she needed the information from this conversation; it was the only way that she could find inner peace.

Finally he spoke.

"I don't know how I feel, it's been really overwhelming that you are here with these messages; but I know they are real. He has done it before with other friends of mine, but I feel it's a lot. You are bringing a lot to me, especially by coming here to Rome with these messages".

She started to cry a lot, driving.

"Please look at the road, you're driving like an Italian woman".

She got really mad now.

"Don't tell me what to do, and you are not the only reason why I'm here in Rome, you know. How dare you! You know, that I have a thing about Rome and that my connection with Angelo is something that came later, and I have been feeling really awful about it. I hate it every time there is a new message for you, because I don't like to pass it on and I don't like letting him down either. I hate that I'm in between you guys. And the worst part is, that he had taught me how to open up my heart, looking like a complete idiot in love, but I just had this love for you and with that came an angel".

"Sorry, I mean it is just so much".

"I know, I think it's too much as well. And I just loved an angel. I just wanted to be there for his and your soul. I have hated to be a part of it, even if I think it's the most beautiful thing I have ever experienced. I have tried to leave so many times, but the part of me that had to learn from it couldn't. I had to stay, even though I looked like a fool so many times".

"I know, I just don't know how to handle it".

She paused, took a deep breath. The words came slowly, in a whisper.

"I'm letting go, it's time..."

His silence answered everything.
The tears went on.

Letting go.
Two words
So easy to say.
So hard to do.
Two words.
With such
A light
Energy
Bringing in
A goodbye.
A new beginning.
Something
Closes.
Something
Opens.
Letting go.
You touch
My body.
You touch
My soul.
I know
It's time for me
To let go.

NINETEEN

Going Home

"Angelo, please come! I need you to be here now. I can't do this anymore. I'm done. Something fell in place with me, with Luca, with Rome, with you and with love. I feel that I'm done now… Please come… We have learned what there was to learn and I need to let you go. It's time".

She was sitting on her bed in her room in Rome, waiting for him to show. It was not often; in fact she hardly ever had asked him to come. But this time she really needed him. She needed him and his blessing so they could let go: she needed a goodbye. It was as if the love she had felt for Luca had formed a journey where she could heal the part of her soul that wanted to learn how to love. Angelo had guided her not to leave before her inner pain had been faced. He had shown her the strength and vulnerability to open up her heart, to stay, to observe even though there was no apparent reason for doing so. She sat for a moment feeling empty, tired as you can only be at the end of a journey. It had felt like a lifetime, but really it was not.

"Ciao Bella".
"Ciao Angelo".
"Thank you for coming, I was scared that you couldn't hear me".

He smiled at her, she could clearly see him this time, his face, his big round face, dark brown eyes and dark brown hair. He was so beautiful; she could see the stars in his eyes, the soft smile on his lips. He was his wise self today. He came with a deep peace.

"I can always hear you, you know that".
"Yes I do, but it doesn't mean that you will show up".
"I know… but you also know that I am aware this is important".

She smiled, she knew that he understood, she was very moved by the situation, she was going to say goodbye. She knew it was the right decision; the pain in her had suddenly and without any specific reason vanished. It was the journey in Rome, with Luca and with Angelo that had in some way healed it. She could not pin point what it was, only that in her a deep peace had occurred.

"I want to let go of you, I want to say good bye, please don't ask me to stay anymore, because I can't, the journey is done".
"Yes I know and I won't ask you to. We have been on such a beautiful journey together. I'm so proud of you. You have a very beautiful heart".

"So do you. You are so magnificent. I have never in my life thought that I would experience something like this. You have been a huge gift in my life, my heart".

"You are amazing. You have such courage to be and explore your pain".

"Thank you, so you are okay with us letting go?"

"Yes, of course. Everything is just temporary. Everything has an end".

"I know. I love you my Italian Angel".

"I love you".

He smiled, touched her face, and touched the tears running down her cheeks. She touched his cheeks. Then he was gone.

An emptiness so big filled her body, and a peace so deep filled the space inside her. In that moment she felt the true rightness of letting him go. It was now time to go home.

My Italian Angel.
My sacred guidance.
Off you go.
Never to
Forget
The journey
We had.
The wisdom
You gave.
The heart
You showed.
The courage
You demanded.
The intensity
You insisted.
The love

You brought.
My heart
Is all
New.
Thank you!
My Italian Angel.

Katrin went into the kitchen and made herself a nice cup of tea, then sat outside on the balcony and watched Rome. She heard the sounds more intensely than ever, watched the skies more closely than ever, tasted the taste of tea more than ever and smelled Rome more than ever. Such was her gratefulness and peace, she now felt Rome's grace and beauty within her: something she had not experienced for many, many years. Not since she had decided that she had fucked up her soul.

Now she was wondering if it was really possible to fuck up your soul? Or if she had just created a situation within her for growth. Who knew really? Who is right? Who has the right answer? Everyone seemed to be fighting to be the one with all the answers. But in the end maybe it just doesn't even matter. We all end up leaving the planet anyway.

She took her cup, washed it in the sink then put it back in place. Everything seemed so silent and slow, like only an ending could do.

She took a long bath, filled it with a lot of soap and with her favorite Lavender Oil that made her relax deeply. Listed to the some relaxing music, her mind flashed back to all events she had experienced in Rome. Luca, Angleo, Caterina and Maria just to mention the most important ones. She knew it was her final night in Rome. She was packing up. Tonight was her time to let it all in, feel it all.

She got up. Put on her bathrobe and went out to the kitchen and got a good glass of wine. Sat in the late afternoon sun, closed her eyes and let her self be.

She had been to her favorite restaurant the night before, dressed up in her nicest dress. She wanted to make a contribution to Rome, a deep gratitude for healing her. They had done it together. She had eaten her favorite food and drunk her favorite wine. Saying goodbye.

She glanced back at the room closing the door slowly, leaving a chapter behind. Took her suitcase and walked down the stairs. The driver was waiting for her. She said her final goodbye on the ride to the airport. A feeling of ease arose in her body.

She checked in, bought a cup of coffee and felt for the first time, that her flight back was greater than ever.

She texted her friend "I'm done here. I'm going home." For the first time in her life, she thought of Denmark as home. She had found a very important part of her and now she was going home.

The plane lifted into the night, leaving Rome behind.

Ciao, Ciao
Dear Rome.
Thank you
For your
Wisdom
Heart
Truth
Craziness

Obsession
An angel
Love.
You have
Given me
My heart.
You left my
Pain in
The space
Between you
And infinity.
I'm full of
Gratitude
And now
I
Fly
Into the skies
Going home.

TWENTY

A Wrap

She sat for a while dozing off. The sun was leaving the day behind. I'm going home, I actually did it. God… it has taken time!

"Do you want some tea?"
"Yes please and a piece of chocolate".
"Thank you".

She drank her tea and a string of thoughts captured her brain in a contemplative mode.

She felt that the journey of love had taught her what the essence of love was. By being and giving instead of receiving. An angel had helped her to stay in Rome and not give up on learning how to love unconditionally. If he hadn't been there, she would probably have lost direction way before and gone home looking like a fool, but he had been the unexpected teacher of loving someone. It was magic.

She felt she had come home for the first time in her life. Felt she was her true self, not lost in the big world. From now on home would be wherever she was, she no longer needed to search and look outside herself anymore. The journey of love had taught her to get back to herself.

In the end she had found the greatest love was experienced through daring to live life, and see life as it really is. To accept the people she loved for what they were, embrace all relationships in whatever form they may take and understand that time delivers lessons to be understood and then released.

Now it was time for her to be whole again, and to share all that divine love with someone. She closed her eyes and fell asleep to the engines breath. Thank God for airplanes and angels.

Despite
The learning
The philosophy
The spirituality
About what love is
What to be
How to set free
Let go
Support the unknown
Always
With an open heart

In the end
It always comes
Down to the
Fact

That sharing love
Is an act
An act of action
Your hearts
Intention
To share
An act
Upon it's wishes
With others
It's what makes
Us Human.

About the Author

This is Lotte Søs Farran-Lee's first novel in a line of upcoming titles in the same series. She is based in Denmark and has a passion for love, travel and living life to her fullest potential every second of her day. She is a writer, therapist, publisher and mom. Follow her blog lotterfarranlee.com

Other upcoming titles by the Author

He doesn't follow the script.
Read more about Michael and Katrin…
would they met again?

It is said that there is a script.

Follow the diary news on
Lottefarranlee.com

Connect with

Author Lotte Søs Farran-Lee on

Blog: www.lottefarranlee.com

Facebook: https://www.facebook.com/lottefarranlee/

And Twitter: @LotteFarranLee

Printed in the United States
By Bookmasters